Ad Blocking Survival Guide

Tactics and Strategies for Web Publishers

The Ad Blocking Survival Guide – First Edition

ISBN-13: 978-1530899005

© 2016 Neil Smyth/eBookFrenzy. All Rights Reserved.

This book is provided for personal use only. Unauthorized use, reproduction and/or distribution strictly prohibited. All rights reserved.

The content of this book is provided for informational purposes only. Neither the publisher nor the author offers any warranties or representation, express or implied, with regard to the accuracy of information contained in this book, nor do they accept any liability for any loss or damage arising from any errors or omissions.

This book contains trademarked terms that are used solely for editorial purposes and to the benefit of the respective trademark owner. The terms used within this book are not intended as infringement of any trademarks.

Rev 1.0

eBookFrenzy

Contents

1. Introduction 1

    1.1 Taking a Measured Approach 2
    1.2 Download the eBook 2
    1.3 Feedback 2
    1.4 Errata 2

2. The State of Online Advertising 5

    2.1 What's the DEAL? 6
    2.2 Making Advertising LEAN 7
    2.3 Summary 7

3. An Overview of Ad Blocking Technology 9

    3.1 Different Types of Ad Blocker 9
    3.2 How Ad Blocking Works 9
        3.2.1 Hiding Advertising Elements 9
        3.2.2 Blocking Access to Ad Servers 10
    3.3 Ad Blocker Lists 12
    3.4 Summary 13

4. Basic Ad Blocker Detection 15

    4.1 How Ad Blocker Detection Works 15
    4.2 An Example of Bait Content 15
    4.3 Detecting the Ad Blocker 16
    4.4 Testing the Detector 17
    4.5 Using the BlockAdBlock Script 21
    4.6 Summary 22

5. Assessing the Damage 25

    5.1 Tracking Ad Blocking with PageFair 25
    5.2 Reviewing the PageFair Results 28
    5.3 Tracking Ad Blocking with Google Analytics 28
    5.4 Creating a Google Analytics Account 29
    5.5 Detecting Ad Blocking 29
    5.6 Triggering Google Analytics Events 31
    5.7 Analyzing the Results 32
    5.8 Creating a Segment for Ad Blockers 34
    5.9 Analyzing the Segment Data 37

i

  5.10 Adding and Removing the AdBlockers Segment 38

  5.11 Blocking of Tracking Scripts 39

  5.12 Summary 39

6. Filling Blocked Ads with Ad Reinsertion 41

  6.1 How Ad Reinsertion Works 41

  6.2 Limitations of Ad Reinsertion 42

  6.3 Implementing Ad Reinsertion 42

  6.4 Choosing The Right Content 45

  6.5 Monitoring the Reinserted Content 45

  6.6 Summary 46

7. Using JavaScript Obfuscation 47

  7.1 What is JavaScript Obfuscation? 47

  7.2 How JavaScript Obfuscation Works 48

  7.3 JavaScript Obfuscation vs. Minifying 49

  7.4 JavaScript Obfuscation and Ad Blocking 49

  7.5 How to Obfuscate JavaScript Code 50

  7.6 Summary 50

8. Seeking Revenue beyond Advertising 51

  8.1 Sell Digital Goods 51

  8.2 Sell Physical Merchandise 52

  8.3 Make Donation Requests 53

  8.4 Build a Mailing List 53

  8.5 Targeting your Email List with Facebook Advertising 53

  8.6 Targeting your Audience with the Facebook Pixel 54

  8.7 Charge for Premium Content 56

  8.8 Charge Visitors for an Ad Free Experience 56

  8.9 Sell Advertising and Sponsorship Direct 56

  8.10 Expand Beyond the Website 57

  8.11 Summary 57

9. Asking Visitors to Turn Off Ad Blocking 59

  9.1 Asking Politely 59

  9.2 Revising Ad Quality, Quantity and Placement 60

  9.3 The EasyList Adblock Warning Removal List 60

  9.4 Displaying a Notification Bar 61

  9.5 Displaying a Dialog Request 64

  9.6 Showing the Dialog and Responding to Button Clicks 67

  9.7 Adding Tracking Code 68

    9.8 Implementing a Timeout Delay 68

    9.9 Summary 71

10. Controlling Ad Blocker Removal Request Frequency 73

    10.1 Deciding on Request Frequency 73

    10.2 An Introduction to Cookies 74

    10.3 What is a JavaScript Cookie? 74

    10.4 The Structure of a Cookie 75

        10.4.1 Cookie Name / Value Pair 75

        10.4.2 Cookie Expiration Setting 75

        10.4.3 Cookie path Setting 75

        10.4.4 Cookie domain Setting 75

    10.5 Configuring Expiration-based Requests 76

    10.6 Displaying the Request Based on Page Views 77

    10.7 Offer a Less Ad Intensive Experience 79

    10.8 Summary 79

11. Denying Website Access to Ad Blocking Visitors 81

    11.1 Does this Approach Work? 81

    11.2 Use with Caution 82

    11.3 Denying Access when Ad Blocking is Enabled 82

    11.4 Offer a Less Ad Intensive Experience 84

    11.5 Summary 84

12. Tracking the Visitor Response Rate 85

    12.1 How the Tracking Works 85

    12.2 Preparing for Tracking Implementation 86

    12.3 Implementing the Tracking Code 86

    12.4 Reviewing the Results 89

    12.5 Summary 90

13. Truncating Web Page Content 91

    13.1 Truncated Content 91

    13.2 Truncating the Content 92

    13.3 Adding the Ad Blocker Whitelist Request 94

    13.4 Implementing the Fading Effect 95

    13.5 Summary 98

14. Participating in the Acceptable Ads Initiative 99

    14.1 The Acceptable Ads Initiative 99

    14.2 The Acceptable Ads Controversy – A Publisher's Friend or Foe? 100

14.3 Are Acceptable Ads an Acceptable Option? ... 101
14.4 Acceptable Ads ... 101
    14.4.1 Placement Criteria ... 101
    14.4.2 Size Criteria ... 102
    14.4.3 Content Criteria ... 102
    14.4.4 Ads Not Considered to be Eligible ... 102
14.5 Getting your Ads Approved ... 103
14.6 Keeping Track of the Results ... 103
14.7 Summary ... 104

15. Running Acceptable Ads with PageFair ... 105

15.1 What is PageFair? ... 105
15.2 How to Run PageFair Ads ... 105
15.3 PageFair Network Ads ... 107
15.4 Running Your Own Ads ... 108
15.5 PageFair Pros and Cons ... 109
15.6 Summary ... 110

16. Running Native Advertising ... 111

16.1 What is Native Advertising? ... 111
16.2 Types of Native Ad Content ... 112
    16.2.1 In-Feed Ads ... 112
    16.2.2 Search Ads ... 113
    16.2.3 Recommendation Widgets ... 113
    16.2.4 Promoted Listings ... 114
    16.2.5 In-Ad ... 115
16.3 Implementing Native Advertising ... 115
16.4 Summary ... 116

17. An Overview of BlockAdBlock, AdSorcery and AdBlock X ... 117

17.1 BlockAdBlock ... 117
17.2 AdSorcery ... 118
17.3 AdBlock X ... 120
17.4 Summary ... 122

18. Useful WordPress Plugins ... 123

18.1 Ad Blocking Detector ... 123
18.2 Ad Blocking Advisor ... 123
18.3 AdBlock X ... 124
18.4 BlockAlyzer ... 124
18.5 Summary ... 124

19. Glossary 125

Index 127

Chapter 1

1. Introduction

A recent report compiled by Adobe and PageFair suggests that almost 200 million people now use an ad blocker when browsing the internet, a 41% increase over the preceding 12 month period. This widespread use of ad blocking technology is expected to result in over $20 billion in lost advertising revenue in 2016 alone.

Despite the magnitude of these numbers, the threat of ad blocking is largely an invisible threat to the average web publisher. Unless steps are taken to assess the impact of ad blocking on an individual website, the only sign that ad blocking is an issue is likely to be a decline in advertising revenue. Given that ad revenue tends to fluctuate for a variety of reasons, even this metric can be misleading.

Ad blocking is certainly far from the only challenge faced by web publishers today. The good news, however, is that ad blocking is one of the few areas where web publishers have some control over how to respond to the issue. We can't cure ad blindness, stop ad budgets migrating to Facebook, and whatever is causing revenues from Google AdSense advertising to decline is far beyond our control. What we do control is our own websites and, by extension, how we react to, communicate with and respond to visitors using ad blocking is entirely up to us.

While there is no "one size fits all" solution, the goal of this book is to outline a range of proven strategies designed not only to detect, quantify and mitigate the threat of ad blocking, but also to move beyond advertising as a sole source of revenue.

The chapters in this book cover a variety of options ranging from passive measuring of ad blocking behavior to the more aggressive step of denying access to those visitors using an ad blocker. While no particular strategy is recommended over another, the inherent risks of a particular option are outlined where necessary so that an informed decision can be made about whether the strategy is right for your situation.

Introduction

1.1 Taking a Measured Approach

To a large extent, the issue of ad blocking has evolved into a technological arms race that has already spawned counter-measures with names such as "anti-ad blocker", "anti anti-ad blocker" and "anti-ad blocker killer".

When considering the strategies in this book, it is important to keep in mind that users have installed ad blockers because they do not want distracting and invasive ads on the sites that they like to visit. As web publishers we have a responsibility to respect this point of view and avoid further fueling the arms race by rushing to adopt the most extreme ad blocking counter-measures. Statistics suggest, for example, that many website visitors will willingly whitelist a website if reasonably requested to do so as long as the content is valuable to them and the ad experience does not impose too great a burden.

While there is no certainty that we will ever reach the point where everyone is blocking ads, we also have an obligation to avoid driving the next 200 million people to install an ad blocker. As part of the process of handling ad blocking, take time to reevaluate the quantity, quality and placement of advertisements on your site with a view to improving the overall visitor experience.

As we hope you will come to appreciate as you read this book, ad blocking survival is a rich and diverse discipline that goes far beyond simply finding ways to make visitors view the same type of ads they have already indicated they do not wish to see.

1.2 Download the eBook

Thank you for purchasing the print edition of this book. If you would like to download the eBook version of this book, please email proof of purchase to *feedback@ebookfrenzy.com* and we will provide you with a download link for the book in PDF, ePub and MOBI formats.

1.3 Feedback

We want you to be satisfied with your purchase of this book. If you find any errors in the book, or have any comments, questions or concerns please contact us at *feedback@ebookfrenzy.com*.

1.4 Errata

While we make every effort to ensure the accuracy of the content of this book. Any known issues with the book will be outlined, together with solutions, at the following URL:

http://www.ebookfrenzy.com/errata/adblockingsurvival.html

In the event that you find an error not listed in the errata, please let us know by emailing our technical support team at *feedback@ebookfrenzy.com*. They are there to help you and will work to resolve any problems you may encounter.

2. The State of Online Advertising

As with just about any market driven economy, the online advertising marketplace is based on the concept of supply and demand. As web publishers, however, we sometimes subconsciously invert the supply and demand equation within the context of online advertising. It is all too easy to think of our websites as representing the demand side, requiring ads from our suppliers (in the form of Google AdSense, ad networks and direct advertisers). The reality, of course, is that the advertising space on our websites is actually the supply side (it is, after all, called "inventory" for a reason), with demand taking the form of advertisers looking for places to run their ads.

Many of the challenges facing advertising funded web publishers today are symptoms of a longstanding imbalance in this supply and demand equation. For quite some time now there has been an unhealthy imbalance between supply and demand, the effects of which have contributed to a backlash from internet users in the form of the increased deployment of ad blocking solutions.

As supply outstripped demand, CPM rates dropped. As web publishers made less money per ad impression many websites tried to compensate by displaying more ads per page. Another symptom of this imbalance is the inability of most ad networks to fill all the inventory on a website. This led to the widespread chaining of ad networks where a request to fill an ad space is passed through multiple ad networks until either an ad is available or the end of the chain is reached. Not only did this result in degraded website performance, but the further down the chain the request travelled, the lower the quality of the ad often became.

Further, the trillions of impressions of low CPM ads designed to build brand awareness that were never intended to be clicked have desensitized visitors to the more valuable CPC ads that were, leading to so-called "ad blindness", declining click-through rates and additional pressure to compensate by running more ads per page.

As people began to see re-targeting advertisements for products they had researched on retail websites follow them around the internet, privacy in online advertising has become an additional area of concern (albeit one based on a misunderstanding of how ad retargeting works).

The reasons for the popularity of ad blocking aside, the facts are not in dispute. Websites that track usage generally report that between 20% – 30% of visitors are using an ad blocker. For websites that rely solely on advertising, the percentage of lost revenue typically falls into a similar percentage range.

The web publishing industry is far from doomed, however. As outlined in the remainder of this book, there are many strategies and technologies available for addressing the ad blocking issue. While some web publishers may fall by the wayside, the future will reward those publishers that continue to produce unique and quality content, take informed, intelligent and measured steps to address ad blocking and think beyond advertising as the only way to turn website traffic into revenue.

2.1 What's the DEAL?

The digital advertising industry is represented by the Interactive Advertising Bureau (IAB). The IAB is comprised of members that include most of the major media, publishing and technology companies. A key responsibility of the IAB is defining the technical standards for online advertising. The various standard ad sizes in use today, for example, were originally defined by the IAB.

Unsurprisingly, the IAB has also taken a keen interest in the issue of ad blocking and has devised a recommended approach that is based on the acronym "DEAL":

- **D**etect ad blocking, in order to initiate a conversation.
- **E**xplain the value exchange that advertising enables.
- **A**sk for changed behavior in order to maintain an equitable exchange.
- **L**ift restrictions or Limit access in response to consumer choice.

This approach advocates a measured approach when addressing the issue of ad blocking. The key goals are focused on educating users about the importance of advertising in supporting web content and seeking a change in behavior by users of ad blocking technology. Only as a last step does the IAB suggest imposing restrictions on access for those users continuing to use ad blocking.

In suggesting this approach, the IAB appears to be attempting to avoid the escalating technology arms race between ad blocker developers and the advertising and publishing industry. It is better, the IAB contends, to give users a reason to willingly turn off ad blocking than to develop ways to defeat ad blocking technology (which will, in turn, result in the development of more advanced ad blocking solutions).

2.2 Making Advertising LEAN

With all the discussion surrounding ad blocking it is easy to lose sight of the fact that people use ad blocking because they feel that advertising has degraded the overall user experience of the internet. If the visitors to a website are viewed as customers, then the old adage that "the customer is always right" suggests that something has gone wrong with the way that online advertising has evolved over the years.

Many people believe that online advertising slows down web page loading, drains phone batteries, exhausts mobile data plans, is overly intrusive, delivers malware and invades their privacy. Some of these perceptions are, of course, based on misunderstandings about how the underlying technology works, but most concerns are valid.

In response to these concerns, the IAB has created a new set of advertising standards referenced by the "LEAN" acronym:

- **L**ight. Limited file size with strict data call guidelines.
- **E**ncrypted. Assure user security with https/SSL compliant ads.
- **A**d Choices Support. All ads should support DAA's consumer privacy programs.
- **N**on-invasive/Non-disruptive. Ads that supplement the user experience and don't disrupt it.

The hope is that the standards for LEAN advertising will be both widely adopted and result in ads that are acceptable to internet users. The widespread deployment of LEAN advertising probably won't be enough to make people uninstall their ad blocker, but it may just prevent others from installing one.

2.3 Summary

Online advertising, like any other marketplace, is based on supply and demand. A seemingly infinite supply of ad space has resulted in a decline in revenue for websites that rely on advertising income. As websites added more ads to compensate for declining revenue an unforeseen side effect was the rise in popularity of ad blockers. The IAB, an industry group representing advertisers and media companies recommends a specific approach to dealing with ad blocking, encapsulated by the DEAL acronym. The IAB is also creating new standards for online advertising that advocate lighter weight, secure and non-invasive ads.

3. An Overview of Ad Blocking Technology

Before exploring strategies to address ad blocking, it is first important to gain a basic understanding of the way in which ad blocking works. This chapter will provide an overview of the different forms of ad blocker and outline the key ways in which most ad blocking technology works.

3.1 Different Types of Ad Blocker

The most common and widely used type of ad blocker takes the form of a web browser extension or plugin, invariably available for installation free of charge with just a few clicks. Custom web browsers are also available with built-in ad blocking capabilities.

Ad blocking within enterprise networks is often implemented using software or hardware devices that are installed within or alongside gateway internet routers.

In addition, some mobile network and internet service providers are considering implementing ad blocking at the network level, thereby stripping out ads from content before it is delivered to customer devices.

3.2 How Ad Blocking Works

Ad blocking typically employs two techniques to eliminate advertising from a web page.

3.2.1 Hiding Advertising Elements

A web page is actually a document that describes how the page is to be rendered within the web browser window. It contains the text, formatting directives, scripts and images that make up the content and behavior of the page that is to be presented to the user.

Browser-based ad blocking is centered around the Document Object Model (DOM). The DOM provides a structured representation of the content of the web page together with a programming interface allowing the content to be accessed and changed. It is the DOM, for

An Overview of Ad Blocking Technology

example, that enables the interactive nature of web pages to be implemented, such as hiding and showing sections of a web page based on user selections, or dynamically changing the style or color of different page elements.

Either before or after the web page loads (depending on the browser type), ad blockers scan the web page document using the DOM to identify any content elements that contain advertising. When ad related content is identified, the DOM programming interface is used to hide those elements from view.

The diagram shown in Figure 3-1 illustrates ad elements hidden by an ad blocker in the form of a web browser extension:

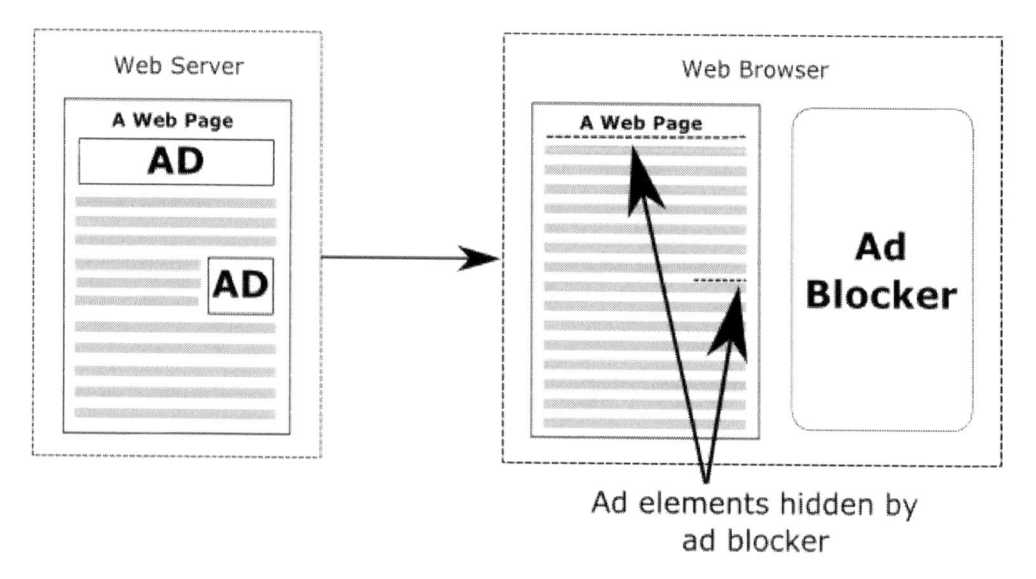

Figure 3-1

3.2.2 Blocking Access to Ad Servers

When a web page containing ads loads into the browser, it contains JavaScript code designed to contact the ad servers that provide the ad content to be displayed. The second technique used by ad blockers involves preventing the browser from contacting those ad servers, thereby preventing the ad from being downloaded and displayed to the user.

Though the exact techniques differ from one web browser type to another, all browsers provide some mechanism for blocking access to external resources such as ad servers. Ad blockers simply use these mechanisms to ensure that any attempt to communicate with a known ad server is blocked (Figure 3-2).

An Overview of Ad Blocking Technology

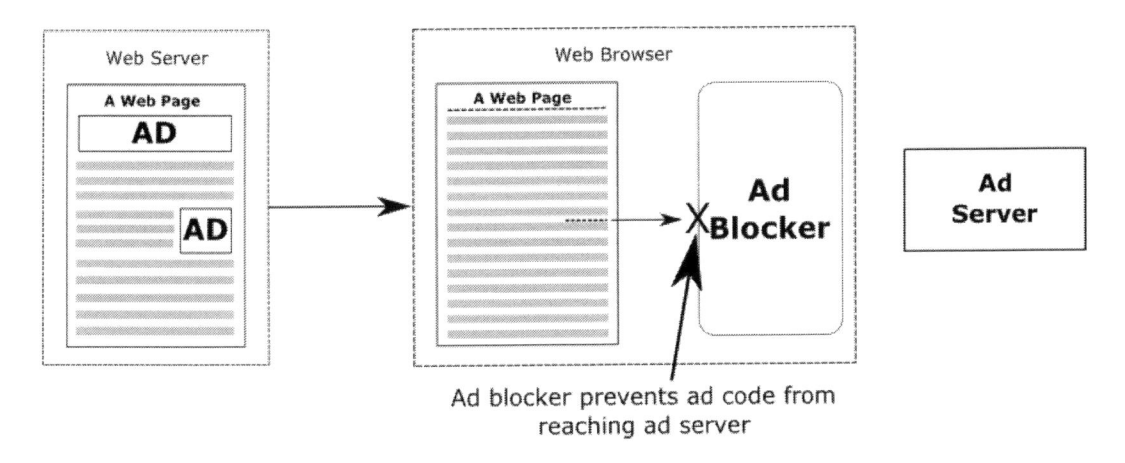

Figure 3-2

The providers of network level ad blocking offer less detail about how their technology works, though it is likely that a combination of hindering ad server communication and on-the-fly modification of web page content prior to delivery of the page to the user's device are employed to provide similar results.

To see this technique in action, install an ad blocker extension into your web browser of choice and enable it. Display the JavaScript console for the browser using the appropriate steps from the following table:

Browser	Steps to Display Console
Google Chrome	Ctrl-Shift-J
Firefox	Ctrl-Shift-J
Internet Explorer	F12
Microsoft Edge	F12
Safari	Select Safari -> Preference menu. Click on the Advanced Tab. Enable "Show Develop menu in menu bar". Press Option-Command-C.

Once the JavaScript console is visible, navigate to a web page containing ads and note the output that appears in the JavaScript console. Among other errors, each blocked attempt to connect with an ad server will be reported within the console. Figure 3-3, for example, shows a list of blocked ad server connections within the JavaScript console of the Chrome web browser:

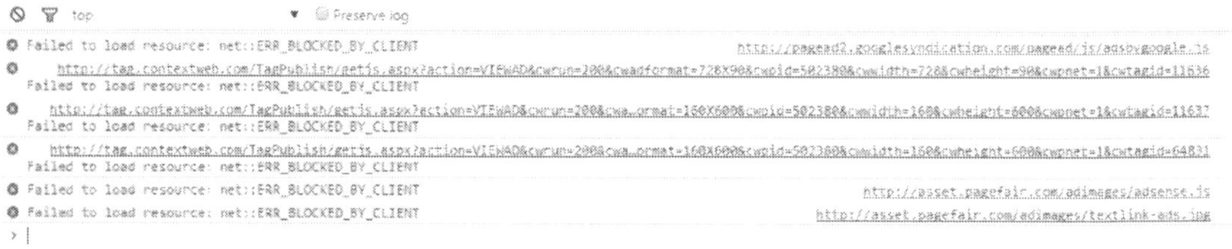

[Screenshot of browser console showing multiple "Failed to load resource: net::ERR_BLOCKED_BY_CLIENT" errors]

Figure 3-3

3.3 Ad Blocker Lists

Having covered how ad blockers hide ads and block ad server communication, the question that remains as to how they know what to block and what to leave alone. This is achieved primarily through the use of filter lists (also referred to as blacklists) which contain sequences of patterns designed to match all of the ad server addresses and web page element names that are known to contain ads. The most widely used filter list is EasyList which is used by the AdBlock Plus ad blocker. The content of this file can be reviewed using the following URL:

https://easylist-downloads.adblockplus.org/easylist.txt

The list contains, for example, the following entry:

```
||contextweb.com^$third-party
```

The web domain contained in the above filter references an ad server used by an online advertising network and inclusion in the list ensures that any attempt by a web page to access this server will be blocked. Similarly, the list contains entries such as the following:

```
##.advert
##.banner_ad
```

These entries dictate that any elements within the web page with class names matching either "advert" or "banner_ad" should be hidden from view. The following <div> element, for example, would be hidden by the ad blocker if encountered in the DOM of a web page:

```
<div class="advert">
    // Ad code here
</div>
```

In addition to the lists containing filters for ad elements and ad servers, privacy lists are also used to block tracking scripts (such as those used by Google Analytics).

In general these lists are user generated in so far as suggestions for additions to the list are submitted by users of the ad blocking tools. If an ad blocker user visits a page where ads are still visible, the user may pass information about the ad element and ad server to the people who maintain the filter list for that particular ad blocker. One of these maintainers will, subject to reviewing the suggestion, create a filter to block the ad and append it to the list.

3.4 Summary

Before addressing the issue of ad blocking it is helpful to first gain an understanding of how ad blocking technology usually works. Ad blockers take a variety of forms including web browser extensions, software solutions and hardware devices.

Ad blocking typically uses two techniques to eliminate advertisements. The first involves the identification of ad elements within a web page and, using the Document Object Model (DOM), hiding those elements from view. The second part of the process involves blocking any attempt by the ad code within a web page to connect to the ad server to obtain the ad content.

Many ad blockers (particularly those provided in the form of a web browser extension) access filter lists to identify the content elements to hide and ad server addresses to block.

Chapter 4

4. Basic Ad Blocker Detection

Just about every strategy for dealing with ad blocking begins with identifying when it is happening. This involves adding to the pages of a website some JavaScript code designed to detect when changes have been made to the page content by an ad blocker.

This chapter will outline the ways in which ad blocker detection typically works before introducing two options for implementing this detection within the pages of a website.

4.1 How Ad Blocker Detection Works

As described in detail in the previous chapter, ad blockers work by blocking communication with the servers providing the ads, and by hiding the elements of web pages that contain advertising content. Ad blockers obtain information about what to block by referring to filter lists containing the addresses of all known ad servers and vast sequences of pattern matching rules.

Ad blocking detection works by placing so-called "bait content" within the pages of a website. Although invisible to the user (it might, for example, be a single pixel in size), this bait content is implemented so as to appear to ad blockers as advertising content. After the web page has finished loading, the detection code checks the properties of the bait content to ascertain whether it is still visible. If the bait content has been hidden, the detection code knows that an ad blocker is active.

4.2 An Example of Bait Content

The following web page element will, if encountered by an ad blocker, be treated as advertising content and hidden from view:

```
<div class="banner_ad"> </div>
```

In terms of the content displayed by the above element, all that this consists of is a single space character. What draws the attention of most ad blockers is the class name of "banner_ad" which can be found within most ad blocker blacklists. This can be verified by opening a browser window and loading the EasyList filter list used by a number of ad blocking extensions, the URL for which is as follows:

Basic Ad Blocker Detection

https://easylist-downloads.adblockplus.org/easylist.txt

Within the list, a search for *banner_ad* should list number of matches, more than one of which will be a perfect match for the bait content outlined above.

4.3 Detecting the Ad Blocker

The most basic of ad blocking detector code simply accesses the bait element and performs a range of tests to identify if the content is still visible. The following JavaScript code, for example, obtains a reference to the banner ad element before checking the height and width properties. If these are set to zero the function makes the reasonable assumption that an ad blocker has hidden the content:

```
<script src=
 "https://ajax.googleapis.com/ajax/libs/jquery/1.12.0/jquery.min.js">
</script>
<script>
(function() {

        var detector = function() {
            setTimeout(function() {

                if(!document.getElementsByClassName) return;
                var ads =
                    document.getElementsByClassName('banner_ad'),
                    ad = ads[ads.length - 1];

                if(!ad || ad.innerHTML.length == 0
                            || ad.clientHeight === 0) {
                    console.log('Ad Blocker Detected');
                } else {
                    console.log('No Ad Blocker');
                }
            }, 2000);
        }

        /* Add a page load listener */
        if(window.addEventListener) {
            window.addEventListener('load', detector, false);
        }
})();
</script>
```

Note that the above code listing includes the following lines of JavaScript:

```
if(window.addEventListener) {
    window.addEventListener('load', detector, false);
}
```

These lines of code configure the browser to call the "detector" function when the web page has finished loading. A closer inspection of the lines of JavaScript code within the detector function will reveal that the JavaScript *setTimeout()* function is used to ensure that the test of the banner ad properties takes place after a 2000 millisecond timeout. The purpose of this delay is to allow the ad blocker to complete its work before checking the status of the banner ad.

As currently implemented, the code simply outputs a message to the browser's JavaScript console to indicate whether an ad blocker has been detected.

4.4 Testing the Detector

If you have access to the server on which your website is running, create a sample html file to test out the above detection code. For example:

```
<html>
<head>
<title>Detector Test Page</title>
</head>
<body>
<h1>Testing the Detector</h1>

<div class="banner_ad"> </div>
<script src=
"https://ajax.googleapis.com/ajax/libs/jquery/1.12.0/jquery.min.js">
</script>
<script>
(function() {

        var detector = function() {
            setTimeout(function() {

                if(!document.getElementsByClassName) return;
                var ads =
                    document.getElementsByClassName('banner_ad'),
                ad  = ads[ads.length - 1];
```

Basic Ad Blocker Detection

```
            if(!ad || ad.innerHTML.length == 0
                       || ad.clientHeight === 0) {
                console.log('Ad Blocker Detected');
            } else {
                console.log('No Ad Blocker');
            }

        }, 2000);
    }

    /* Add a page load listener */
    if(window.addEventListener) {
        window.addEventListener('load', detector, false);
    }
})();
</script>
</body>
</html>
```

Alternatively, if you are using a WordPress installation select the *Appearance* option from the WordPress dashboard followed by the *Editor* entry as illustrated in Figure 4-1 below (note that these options are not available for sites hosted on WordPress.com):

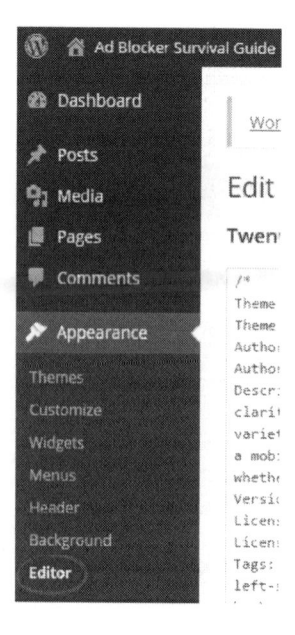

Figure 4-1

From the drop down menu in the upper right hand corner of the main panel, select the theme you are using for your website and click on the Select button:

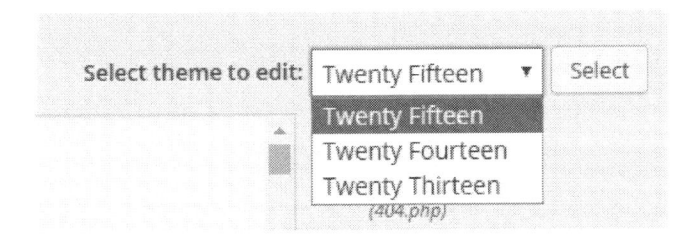

Figure 4-2

Next, select the Footer (footer.php) entry from the *Templates* list located on the right hand side of the page as shown in Figure 4-3:

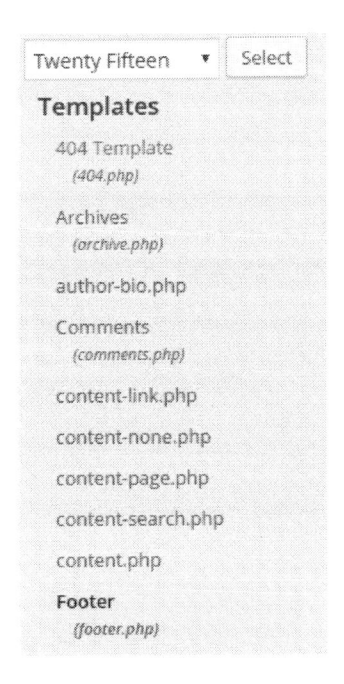

Figure 4-3

Within the code for the template, scroll down until the </body> tag comes into view and place the bait ad and detection JavaScript code immediately above it:

Basic Ad Blocker Detection

```
?>
            </div><!-- .site-content -->

            <footer id="colophon" class="site-footer" role="contentinfo">
                <div class="site-info">
                    <?php
                        /**
                         * Fires before the Twenty Fifteen footer text for
footer customization.
                         *
                         * @since Twenty Fifteen 1.0
                         */
                        do_action( 'twentyfifteen_credits' );
                    ?>
                    <a href="<?php echo esc_url( __( 'https://wordpress.org/',
'twentyfifteen' ) ); ?>"><?php printf( __( 'Proudly powered by %s', 'twentyfifteen'
), 'WordPress' ); ?></a>
                </div><!-- .site-info -->
            </footer><!-- .site-footer -->

</div><!-- .site -->

<?php wp_footer(); ?>

            ⬅ Paste Code Here

</body>
</html>
```

Figure 4-4

Once the code has been added, click on the *Update File* button. If the button is not visible or WordPress indicates the file cannot be saved, follow the steps on the following page to add write permission to the *footer.php* file:

https://codex.wordpress.org/Changing_File_Permissions

The path to the file for which permissions need to be changed will be as follows (where *<theme name>* is replaced by the name of the theme you are using on your site):

```
wp-content/themes/<theme name>/footer.php
```

If you are using another content management system such as Joomla! or Drupal, refer to the documentation for steps on embedding JavaScript code into the web pages of your site.

Once the detector code has been added, open a browser in which an ad blocker extension is installed and display the JavaScript console using the steps outlined in the chapter entitled *An Overview of Ad Blocking Technology*.

With the console displayed, load a web page containing the detector code while the ad blocker extension is disabled and verify that the "No Ad Blocker" message appears (keeping in mind that there will be a 2000 millisecond delay before the message appears). Enable the ad blocker, reload the page and check the console for the appearance of the "Ad Blocker Detected" message.

See it in Action

http://www.techotopia.com/survival/detect.html

4.5 Using the BlockAdBlock Script

The above example provides a simple approach to detecting ad blockers and offers an insight into the way in which such detection typically works. A number of different detection scripts are also freely available for download from a variety of websites. Many of these are similar to the example outlined previously in this chapter. For a more robust and extensive detection option, the BlockAdBlock script is a well-regarded alternative that is widely used within the web publisher community. Details of this script and download instructions are available at the following URL:

https://github.com/sitexw/BlockAdBlock

To implement BlockAdBlock, download the *blockadblock.js* file from the above web page and install it onto your web server. Next, add the following to each web page for which detection is required:

```
<script src="/blockadblock.js"></script>

<script>
// Function called if AdBlock is not detected
function adBlockNotDetected() {
    console.log('Ad Blocker Detected');
}
// Function called if AdBlock is detected
function adBlockDetected() {
    console.log('No Ad Blocker');
}

// Recommended audit because AdBlock locks the file 'blockadblock.js'
```

```
// If the file is not called, the variable does not exist
'blockAdBlock'
// This means that AdBlock is present
if(typeof blockAdBlock === 'undefined') {
    adBlockDetected();
} else {
    blockAdBlock.onDetected(adBlockDetected);
    blockAdBlock.onNotDetected(adBlockNotDetected);
}
</script>
```

In addition to containing countermeasures to avoid itself being blocked by ad blockers, the BlockAdBlock script also removes the bait after detection and includes a range of configuration options not available with simpler scripts. Configuration options are available to output debug information to the JavaScript console, control whether the ad blocker detection check is performed automatically when the web page loads and configuration of the number of times the detection is performed and the duration between each attempt. The following code, for example, enables debugging output and disables detection at web page load time:

```
blockAdBlock.setOption({
    debug: true,
    checkOnLoad: false
});
```

If the checkOnLoad option is set to false, the detection can be triggered independently from anywhere within the web page via a call to the blockAdBlock.check() function as follows:

```
<script>
  .
  .

        blockAdBlock.check()
  .
  .
</script>
```

4.6 Summary

The first step in dealing with ad blocking involves identifying when it is taking place. This involves placing bait content (essentially a page element known to be identified as an advertisement by an ad blocker) and some JavaScript detection code. The web page is then configured to call the detection code a short time after the web page has loaded. The detection code inspects properties of the bait content to verify if it is still visible. If the bait is hidden then the presence of an ad blocker is assumed.

5. Assessing the Damage

The extent to which ad blocking impacts a website will vary from one site to another and is often dictated primarily by audience demographics. Current trends suggest that websites appealing to a younger or more technically oriented audience are likely to encounter a greater percentage of ad blocking activity than other types of website.

The first step in considering how to mitigate the effects of ad blocking, therefore, is to identify not only whether the problem exists, but that it does so to the extent that further action is justified. If only 10% of visitors to a website are using an ad blocker, for example, the website owner may reasonably make the judgement that the effort involved in adapting to the threat outweighs the benefits. To make this an informed decision, however, it is first necessary to gather and analyze website visitor behavior data.

The focus of this chapter, therefore, is to outline some steps that can be taken to obtain accurate data on how many visitors to a website have an ad blocker enabled. Two levels of ad blocker tracking will be introduced in this chapter. The first provides a simpler approach using a free service provided by PageFair (another free service, AdBlock X, will also be covered in the chapter entitled *An Overview of BlockAdBlock, AdSorcery and AdBlock X*). The second option makes use of Google Analytics and provides a greater level of detail and data collection options.

5.1 Tracking Ad Blocking with PageFair

For those in a hurry, the path of least resistance to tracking the percentage of ad blocker usage on a website is to sign up for a PageFair account. In addition to providing ad blocker tracking, PageFair also provides an option to generate revenue from some blocked ads, a topic that will be covered later in this book. For the purposes of this chapter, however, only the ad blocker measurement service will be used.

Visit *https://pagefair.com* and create a new account by entering your email address, password and website information. Once signed into PageFair, select the *Setup* tab to locate the ad block detection and measurement JavaScript code as illustrated in Figure 5-1:

Assessing the Damage

```
Basic Setup                                              Enables adblock detection and measurement

Insert this snippet into your website source code, if your site has jQuery leave out the first line.

<script type="text/javascript" src="http://ajax.googleapis.com/ajax/libs/jquery/1.8.1/jquery.min.js"></script>
<script type="text/javascript">
 (function(){
   function async_load(script_url){
     var protocol = ('https:' == document.location.protocol ? 'https://' : 'http://');
     var s = document.createElement('script'); s.src = protocol + script_url;
     var x = document.getElementsByTagName('script')[0]; x.parentNode.insertBefore(s, x);
   }
   bm_website_code = 'A28AA4B4718245F0';
   jQuery(document).ready(function(){async_load('asset.pagefair.com/measure.min.js')});
   jQuery(document).ready(function(){async_load('asset.pagefair.net/ads.min.js')});
 })();
</script>

                                                            Need instructions? [wordpress] [vBulletin]

                              [ Do I have jQuery installed? ]    [ Verify Installation ]
                              (Note: we cannot detect jQuery or the PageFair snippet when inserted by a tag manager.)
```

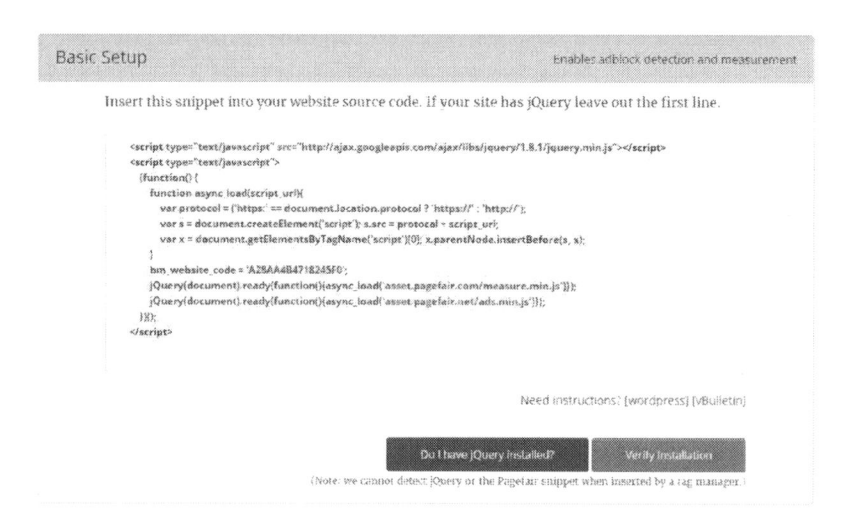

Figure 5-1

The PageFair JavaScript code makes use of the jQuery JavaScript library. If your website already imports this library it will not need to do so again. Before adding the measurement code to your website, click on the *Do I have jQuery installed?* button. If PageFair detects that jQuery is already installed, it is not necessary to include the first line of the code in your web pages.

For WordPress based websites the code can be added via the Theme Editor within the WordPress dashboard. Instructions to achieve this can be viewed by clicking on the WordPress *Need instructions?* link on the PageFair setup screen. For other sites, cut and paste the code into the appropriate location within your website markup so that it is placed between the header <head> and </head> tags and is included in every page for which tracking is required.

If you are using a WordPress installation, select the *Appearance* option from the WordPress dashboard followed by *Editor* as outlined in the previous chapter. From the drop down menu in the upper right hand corner of the main panel, select the theme you are using for your website and click on the Select button.

Next, select the Header (header.php) entry from the *Templates* list located on the right hand side of the page as shown in Figure 5-2:

Assessing the Damage

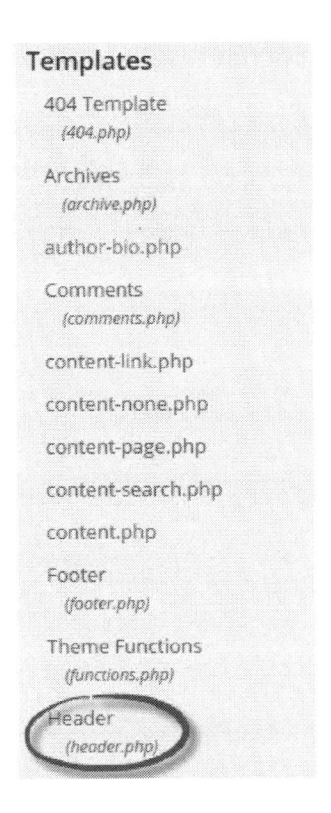

```
Templates
    404 Template
        (404.php)
    Archives
        (archive.php)
    author-bio.php
    Comments
        (comments.php)
    content-link.php
    content-none.php
    content-page.php
    content-search.php
    content.php
    Footer
        (footer.php)
    Theme Functions
        (functions.php)
   (Header)
        (header.php)
```

Figure 5-2

Once the code for the header template is displayed, paste the PageFair code into the template so that it is positioned immediately before the </head> tag:

```
<?php
/**
 * The template for displaying the header
 *
 * Displays all of the head element and everything up until the "site-content" div.
 *
 * @package WordPress
 * @subpackage Twenty_Fifteen
 * @since Twenty Fifteen 1.0
 */
?><!DOCTYPE html>
<html <?php language_attributes(); ?> class="no-js">
<head>
    <meta charset="<?php bloginfo( 'charset' ); ?>">
    <meta name="viewport" content="width=device-width">
    <link rel="profile" href="http://gmpg.org/xfn/11">
    <link rel="pingback" href="<?php bloginfo( 'pingback_url' ); ?>">
    <!--[if lt IE 9]>
    <script src="<?php echo esc_url( get_template_directory_uri() ); ?>/js/html5.js"></script>
    <![endif]-->
    <?php wp_head(); ?>
           <— Paste Code Here
</head>
```

Figure 5-3

Assessing the Damage

Click on the Update File button to save the changes, or follow the steps outlined in the previous chapter to add write permission to the following file (where *<theme name>* is replaced by the name of the WordPress theme you are using):

```
wp-content/themes/<theme name>/header.php
```

Once the code has been added to the website, click on the *Verify Installation* button to check that the code is correctly installed and functioning.

5.2 Reviewing the PageFair Results

It may take up to 24 hours for tracking results to become available within the PageFair dashboard. To view the results, select the *Reports -> Audience* option within the PageFair dashboard to display the data in graph form:

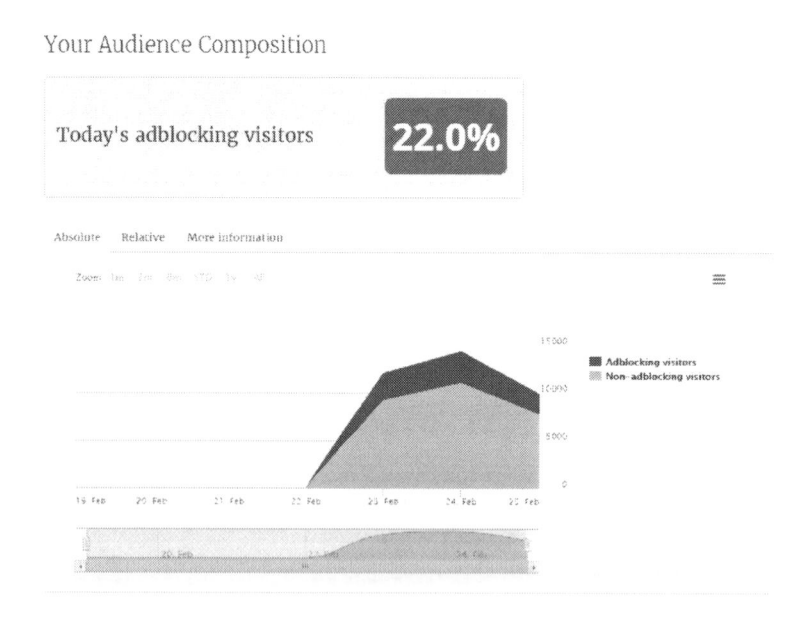

Figure 5-4

The above audience report displays the percentage of ad blocking activity on a per visitor basis. For traffic breakdown based on individual page views, select the *Reports -> Traffic* option.

5.3 Tracking Ad Blocking with Google Analytics

Measuring ad blocking using Google Analytics requires slightly more work than using PageFair but has the advantage of bringing the full power of Google Analytics to bear when measuring ad blocking behavior. Data available within Google Analytics includes the geographical location of visitors, browser and device type in use and the operating system on which the browser is running. The fact that many web publishers already use Google Analytics also makes this an ideal choice for measuring ad blocking activity on a website.

The process of tracking ad blocking behavior within Google Analytics involves adding ad blocker detection code to each website page. This code is designed to trigger a different Google Analytics event depending on whether or not ad blocking is being used by visitors to the site.

5.4 Creating a Google Analytics Account

If you do not already have a Google Analytics account, create one now for free by going to *https://www.google.com/analytics/*, clicking on the "Sign In" link and selecting Google Analytics from the drop down menu. Enter the email address and password associated with your Google account if prompted to do so (or create a Google account if you do not already have one).

Having reached the Google Analytics sign up screen (Figure 5-5) click on the Sign Up button to begin the account creation process.

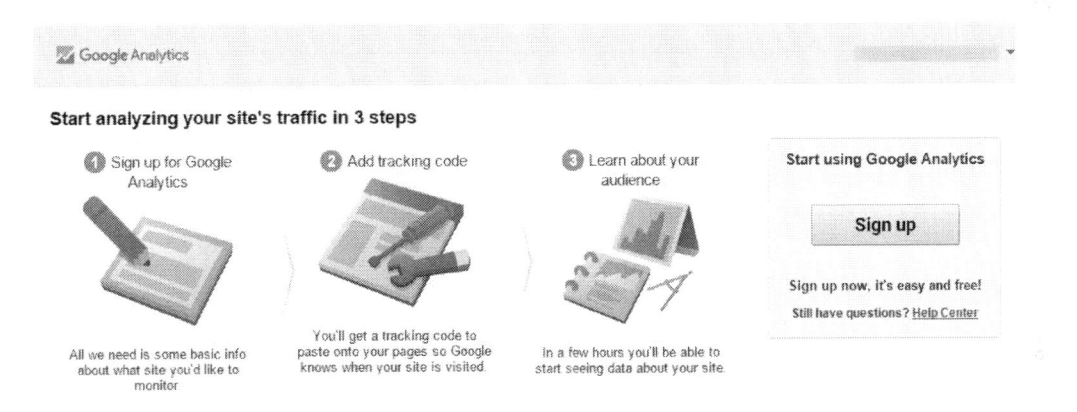

Figure 5-5

On the subsequent New Account form, select the "Website" option and enter the necessary information for your site to configure tracking. Having filled in the appropriate form fields, click on the *Get Tracking ID* button and add the code to your website so that it is included on every page that is to be tracked. If you are using WordPress, follow the steps above to place the code in the <head> section of the theme *header.php* template.

5.5 Detecting Ad Blocking

The next step in implementing ad blocker tracking is to add the detection code to the pages of the website. Once again, this code will need to be present in every page for which tracking is

Assessing the Damage

required. For the purposes of this example, the JavaScript detection code outlined in the chapter entitled *Basic Ad Blocker Detection* will be repurposed to trigger Google Analytics events instead of sending output to the browser's JavaScript console. As outlined in the previous chapter, the sample detection JavaScript code reads as follows:

```
<div class="banner_ad"> </div>
<script src="https://ajax.googleapis.com/ajax/libs/jquery/1.12.0/jquery.min.js"></script>
<script>
(function() {

        var detector = function() {
            setTimeout(function() {

                if(!document.getElementsByClassName) return;
                var ads =
                    document.getElementsByClassName('banner_ad'),
                    ad = ads[ads.length - 1];

                if(!ad || ad.innerHTML.length == 0
                        || ad.clientHeight === 0) {
                    console.log('Ad Blocker Detected');
                } else {
                    console.log('No Ad Blocker');
                }

            }, 2000);
        }

        /* Add a page load listener */
        if(window.addEventListener) {
            window.addEventListener('load', detector, false);
        }
})();
</script>
```

As an initial test, embed the above code into your website so that it appears on every page that is to be tracked. Make sure to place this code so that it is positioned beneath the Google Analytics tracking code added earlier in this chapter.

Assessing the Damage

Display the JavaScript console for your browser (as outlined in the chapter entitled *Basic Ad Blocker Detection*) and load different pages while enabling and disabling the ad blocker. Check the console output to verify that the code correctly detects the presence of an ad blocker by outputting "Ad Blocker Detected" and "No Ad Blocker" messages.

5.6 Triggering Google Analytics Events

Having verified that the code is correctly detecting the presence of an active ad blocker, the code now needs to be enhanced to trigger Google Analytics events. Edit the JavaScript detection code so that it reads as follows:

```
<div class="banner_ad"> </div>
<script src="https://ajax.googleapis.com/ajax/libs/jquery/1.12.0/jquery.min.js"></script>
<script>
(function() {

        var detector = function() {
            setTimeout(function() {

                if(!document.getElementsByClassName) return;
                var ads =
                    document.getElementsByClassName('banner_ad'),
                    ad  = ads[ads.length - 1];

                if(!ad || ad.innerHTML.length == 0
                        || ad.clientHeight === 0) {
                    ga('send', {
                        'hitType': 'event',
                        'eventCategory': 'AdBlocker',
                        'eventAction': 'Blocked',
                        'nonInteraction': 1
                    });

                    console.log('Ad Blocker Detected');
                } else {
                    ga('send', {
                        'hitType': 'event',
                        'eventCategory': 'AdBlocker',
                        'eventAction': 'Not Blocked',
                        'nonInteraction': 1
```

Assessing the Damage

```
                        });

                        ~~console.log('No Ad Blocker');~~
                }
         }, 2000);
      }

      /* Add a page load listener */
      if(window.addEventListener) {
          window.addEventListener('load', detector, false);
      }
})();
</script>
```

The tasks performed by these code changes are quite simple. If an ad blocker is detected, an event is sent to Google Analytics with the event category set to "AdBlocker" and the event action declared as "Blocked". If no ad blocker is detected an "AdBlocker" category event is sent, this time with the event action set to "Not Blocked".

5.7 Analyzing the Results

Although Google Analytics will begin recording and reporting data almost immediately, the amount of time it will take to gather meaningful statistics will vary depending on the volume of traffic to the website.

To view the statistics, open Google Analytics in a browser window and display the reporting information for the website. Within the left hand navigation panel, select *Behavior -> Events -> Top Event* to display information about the AdBlocker event category as highlighted in Figure 5-6:

Assessing the Damage

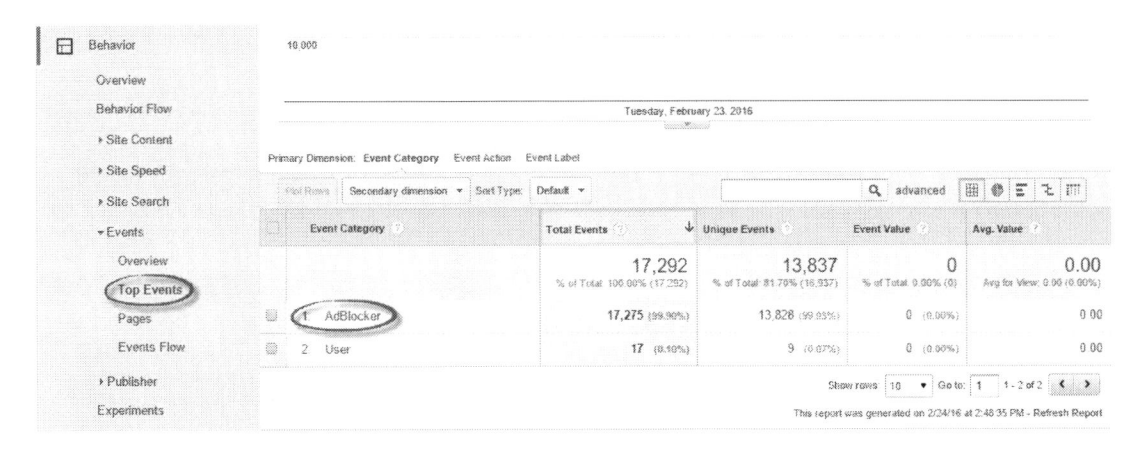

Figure 5-6

Click on the AdBlocker category to view the data for the individual event actions:

Figure 5-7

To access a graphical view of the event actions data, click on one of the buttons located in the right hand side of the toolbar. Figure 5-8, for example, shows the data in the form of a pie chart:

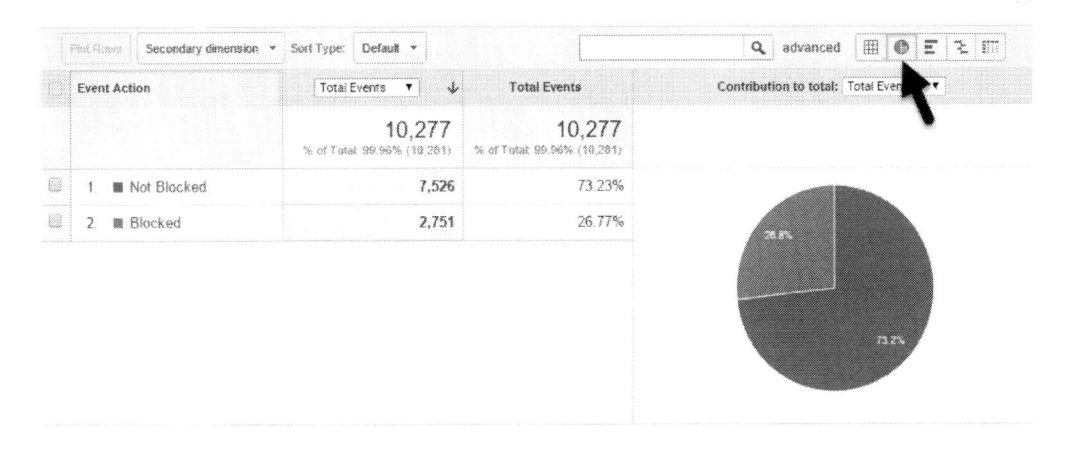

Figure 5-8

Assessing the Damage

Refer to the Total Events column of the table to identify the percentage of visitors using ad blockers during the specified time and date range. To view statistics for different date and time ranges, or to compare one time period with another, use the panel located in the upper right hand corner of the Google Analytics page. In Figure 5-9, for example, a comparison is being configured between two different date ranges:

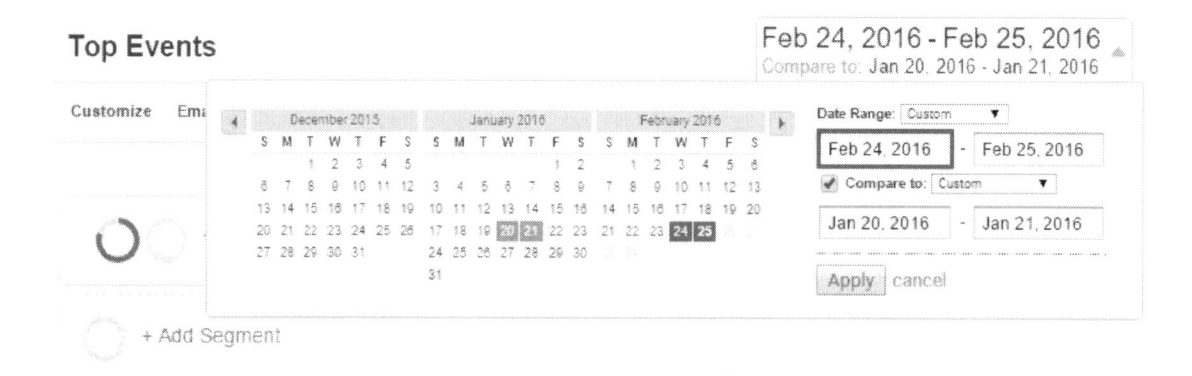

Figure 5-9

5.8 Creating a Segment for Ad Blockers

To gain access to additional information on those visitors using an ad blocker it will be necessary to create a new segment targeting those users. Begin by selecting the *Audience -> Overview* option from the left hand navigation panel and, within the main panel click on "+ Add Segment" as highlighted in Figure 5-10:

Figure 5-10

In the resulting panel, click on the red "+ New Segment" button to display the new segment configuration panel. In the upper section of the panel enter *AdBlockers* into the Segment Name text field before selecting the Conditions option located under Advanced in the navigation panel:

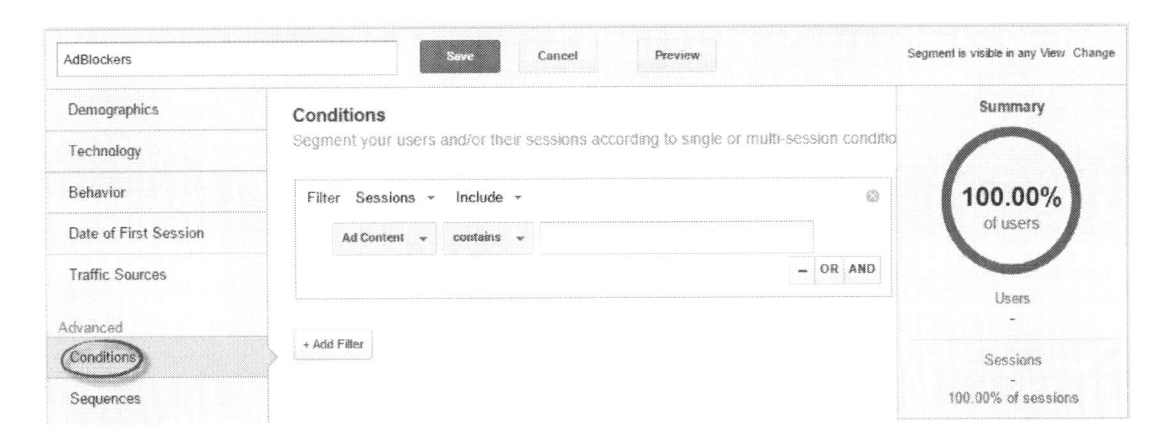

Figure 5-11

The objective here is to configure a new segment that contains visitors who triggered the "Blocked" event action of the "AdBlocker" event category. Within the condition settings, click on the *Ad* Content drop-down menu and enter *event category* into the search box to locate the Event Category entry:

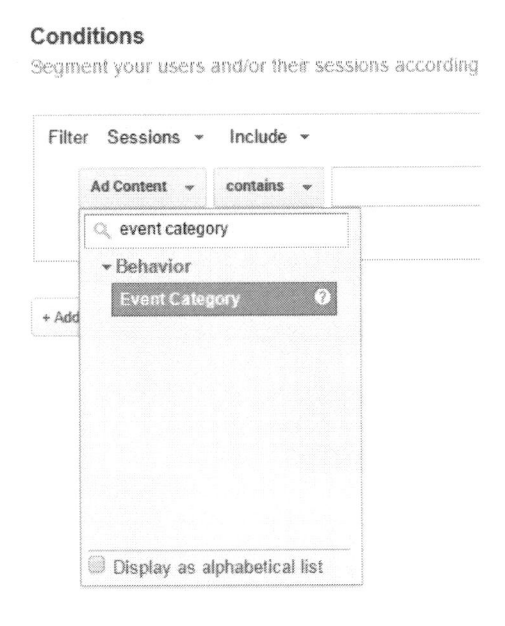

Figure 5-12

Select the Event Category item from the list, change the condition setting to "matches exactly" and enter *AdBlocker* as the category name. At this point the condition filter should match that shown in Figure 5-13:

Assessing the Damage

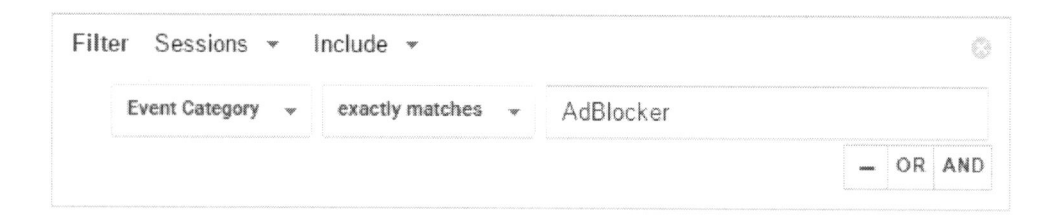

Figure 5-13

As currently configured, the segment will include all visitors that triggered AdBlocker category events regardless of which event action was triggered. The filter needs to be further refined to match only those entries containing a "Blocked" event action. Click on the *AND* button to add another condition to the filter and select the *Ad Content* button in this entry to display the drop-down menu. Enter *event action* into the search box and select the item from the list when it appears:

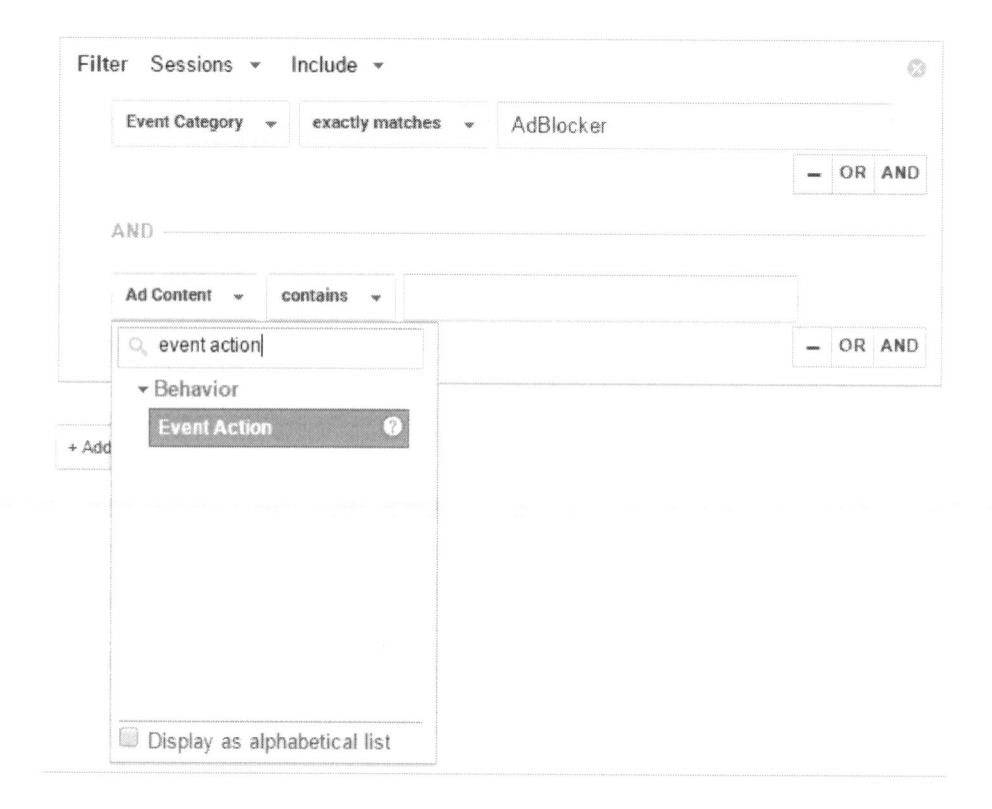

Figure 5-14

Remaining within the second filter configuration, change the condition from *contains* to *matches exactly* and enter *Blocked* into the text field. On completion of these steps the condition filter should read as shown in Figure 5-15:

Figure 5-15

Click on the Save button to commit the changes.

5.9 Analyzing the Segment Data

Once the segment has been saved it will automatically appear in the audience overview results as illustrated in Figure 5-16. This allows the percentage of visitors using ad blockers to be reviewed over different periods of time. Options are also available to compare the results to other time periods to track whether the situation is worsening.

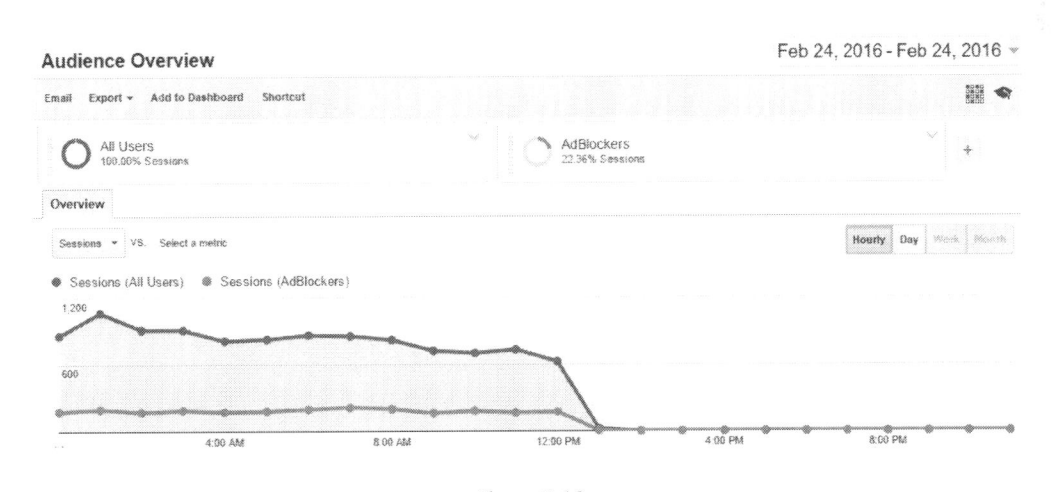

Figure 5-16

Assessing the Damage

Scroll down the page until the demographics section comes into view. Select the *Country* option to view geographical data on visitors using ad blockers:

Demographics	Country	Sessions	% Sessions
Language	1. India		
Country	All Users	2,185	20.34%
City	AdBlockers	281	11.71%
System	2. United States		
Browser	All Users	1,968	18.32%
Operating System	AdBlockers	419	17.46%
Service Provider	3. United Kingdom		
Mobile	All Users	596	5.55%
Operating System	AdBlockers	122	5.08%
Service Provider	4. Germany		
Screen Resolution	All Users	470	4.37%
	AdBlockers	132	5.50%

Figure 5-17

Take time to explore other information such as browser type and operating system. The segment configuration will also provide information in other areas of Google Analytics. This information can be used to gauge the impact of ad blocking on your website advertising revenue. If most of your revenue is generated by customers in the United States, for example, but the majority of visitors using ad blockers are based in another country then the issue may not warrant further action.

Similarly, the operating system data might indicate that most visitors running Android or iOS are not yet using ad blockers. If the majority of your revenue comes from mobile ads then the problem may be less severe than the overall percentage of ad blockers at first suggests.

5.10 Adding and Removing the AdBlockers Segment

To remove the AdBlockers segment from the results within Google Analytics, click on the down arrow in the segment panel as outlined in Figure 5-18 and select the *Remove* option:

Figure 5-18

To reapply the segment to the analysis, click on the *Add Segment* panel and enable the *AdBlockers* check box within the segment list before clicking on the *Apply* button. If the AdBlockers segment data is to be displayed in relation to all other website visitors, be sure to keep the *All Users* option enabled:

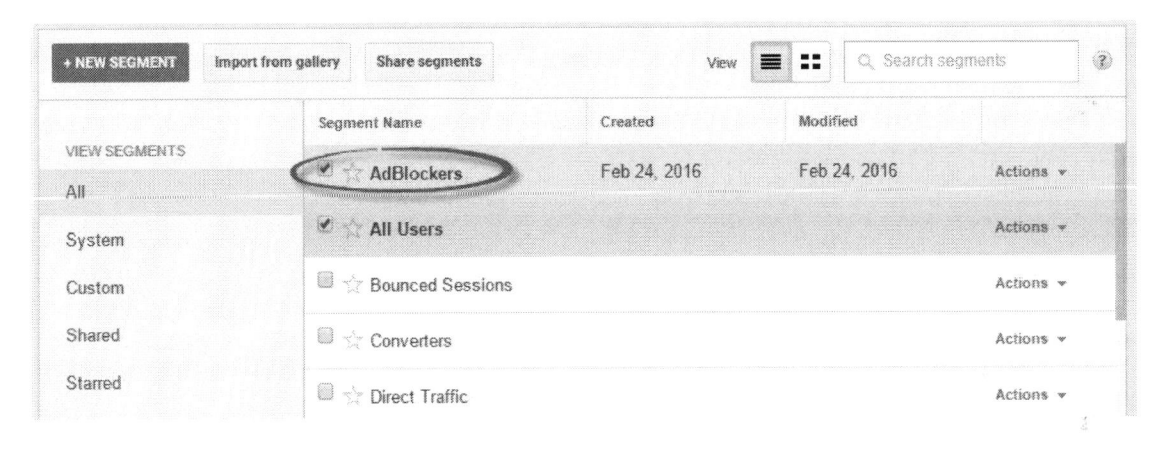

Figure 5-19

5.11 Blocking of Tracking Scripts

It is important to be aware that some ad blockers provide the option to also block tracking scripts such as those provided by PageFair and Google Analytics. It is possible, therefore, that the results gathered using these techniques will not be 100% accurate. That being said, even with some users blocking tracking activity, the data gathered should be a large enough representative sample to provide a reasonably accurate assessment.

5.12 Summary

The impact of ad blocking will vary from one website to another. It is important, therefore, to gauge the level of ad blocking activity as a percentage of overall traffic. A quick assessment can be made using a third-party service such as that offered by PageFair. Alternatively, more in depth

Assessing the Damage

analysis may be performed using Google Analytics, allowing additional data such as geography and platform type to be monitored.

6. Filling Blocked Ads with Ad Reinsertion

At this point in the book we know how to detect and measure the presence of ad blockers when visitors load web pages from a website. This raises the question of what to do about the blocked ads. When an ad blocker is used by site visitors, spaces that once contained revenue generating advertising will either be empty, or will have been filled in by the surrounding content of the web page.

The next step, and the topic of this chapter, is to explore some ways to display alternative content in place of the blocked ads.

6.1 How Ad Reinsertion Works

Ad reinsertion refers to the process of backfilling blocked advertising space on a web page with alternate content. As previously discussed, ad blockers prevent ads from appearing either by blocking communication with ad servers, or by hiding web page elements containing identification patterns that match entries in the ad blocking list (if, for example, a <div> element has a class name of "banner_ad" the ad blocker will hide this element from view).

If an ad has been prevented from appearing by blocking communication with the ad server, and the ad is not embedded in a <div> element that matches any ad blocker list entries, then the now empty element is essentially still displayed on the web page. Not only is this element still visible, it is also accessible to you via JavaScript code. If an element is both visible and accessible, you can write new content to it.

In the chapter entitled *Basic Ad Blocker Detection* we learned how to detected the presence of an ad blocker. In the JavaScript examples provided, the detection code simply outputs a message to the JavaScript console to report the detection of an ad blocker. The concept of reinsertion uses the same technique to detect an ad blocker, but goes one step further by writing new content to the blocked web page elements.

6.2 Limitations of Ad Reinsertion

Before looking at some practical reinsertion implementations, it is important to be aware of the limitations of this strategy:

- An ad space cannot be backfilled with another advertising tag or any content that is delivered by a recognized ad server such as DoubleClick. This code will be blocked when it attempts to connect to the server providing the ad content. Use the space instead to encourage users to turn off ad blocking, or to run house ads to promote other products or services related to the content of your site.
- The original ad must not be contained within an element that will be identified as containing an ad. If it does it will be hidden by the ad blocker, along with any new content written to it. When giving the element that contains the ad an identifier, be sure to use a name that is not contained within any ad blocker lists.
- It will be necessary to change the identifier of the element containing the ad should the current name be added to ad blocker lists in the future.
- Many ad blockers provide users the ability to block individual elements within a web page and there is nothing to stop visitors doing this on reinserted elements. On the positive side, however, the user will not only see your reinserted ad when it first appears, but will also have to right-click on it to access the ad blocker menu option to hide the element. If the ad is compelling and relevant, the visitor may actually click on it instead and make a purchase. Alternatively, include some of the main content from the web page within the same element as the reinserted ad. The visitor will then be unable to hide the ad element without also hiding the content they actually want to see.

6.3 Implementing Ad Reinsertion

For the purposes of an example, consider a simple web page containing a 336x280 Google AdSense ad embedded within a <div> element. The HTML for such an element might read as follows:

```
<div id="mydiv">
<script async
src="//pagead2.googlesyndication.com/pagead/js/adsbygoogle.js">
</script>
<!-- Large 336x280 Rectangle Ad -->
<ins class="adsbygoogle"
     style="display:inline-block;width:336px;height:280px"
     data-ad-client="ca-pub-7393409012121212"
     data-ad-slot="6792121212"></ins>
```

```
<script>
(adsbygoogle = window.adsbygoogle || []).push({});
</script>
</div>
```

When a page containing the above element is loaded into a browser in which an ad blocker is enabled, the Google ad tag will be blocked and no ad will appear. Since the id name assigned to the <div> tag is not contained in any ad blocker blacklists, the element will not be hidden by the ad blocker, thereby leaving it open for alternate content to be displayed.

Using the example ad block detection code outlined in the chapter entitled *Basic Ad Blocker Detection*, code can be implemented to display a house advertisement promoting some other form of revenue generating product or service, or even a donation request. The following code, for example, shows a fragment of the ad blocker detection code from the *Basic Ad Blocker Detection* chapter, this time implemented to reinsert an ad in the mydiv element with an image promoting a T-Shirt hyperlinked directly to a page where a purchase can be made:

```
<script>
.
.
.
if(!ad || ad.innerHTML.length == 0
        || ad.clientHeight === 0) {
    console.log('Ad Blocker Detected');

    $("#mydiv").html('<a href= \
        "https://teespring.com/ios-swift-shirt"> \
         <img src="/images/shirt_image.png"></a>');

    } else {
       console.log('No Ad Blocker');
    }

  }, 2000);
}
.
.
.
</script>
```

When a visitor loads the webpage containing the above code, the blocked ad will appear as illustrated in Figure 6-1:

Filling Blocked Ads with Ad Reinsertion

A Backfill Example

This web page demonstrates a practical implementation of the concept of ad backfilling as outlined in the book "The Ad Blocking Survival Guide." Backfilling occurs when a website detects the presence of an ad blocker and uses the blocked ad elements to display alternate revenue generating content that does not trigger the ad blocker. To see this in effect, try reloading this page both with and without an ad blocker extension enabled.

Support Techotopia
Buy an App Developer T-Shirt

Backfilling can be put to a variety of uses. It can, for example, be used to display in-house advertising or to make an appeal to the site visitor to turn off ad blocking.

Figure 6-1

Ad reinsertion can be used to perform any form of promotional advertising as long as it does not insert content that would be viewed as advertising by an ad blocker. As classic mistake when using reinsertion is to use a blacklisted naming pattern when referencing images or scripts. Consider, for example, the following adaptation of the above example:

```
$("#mydiv").html('<a href= \
   "https://teespring.com/ios-swift-shirt"> \
      <img src="/AdFiles/shirt_image.png"></a>');
```

When the above content is written to the mydiv element it will be blocked because the image pathname contains "AdFile" which the ad blocker will detect as being ad related.

The reinserted content may contain any combination of images and text. Some web publishers simply display a text message within the blocked ad space appealing to visitors to disable ad blocking:

```
$("#mydiv").html('<div style="display: table-cell; \
vertical-align: middle; background-color: orange;"> \
   <div style="text-align:center;  font-size: 250%;"> \
        Keep our content free. Please turn off your ad blocker. \
   </div> \
</div>');
```

Figure 6-2 shows how the above HTML will be rendered when used to backfill a blocked ad:

> Keep our content free. Please consider turning off your ad blocker.

Figure 6-2

6.4 Choosing The Right Content

Clearly just about any content can be used to fill a blocked ad space as long as it does not take the form of an ad tag or any content delivered by an ad server. Wherever possible, however, try to promote products or services that are likely to appeal to your visitor demographic. In the above example, a T-Shirt designed for app developers was posted on a website that provides app development tutorials. This particular ad reinsertion campaign was successful because it promoted a product targeted specifically towards the interests of the site's visitors. Other options for generating revenue from ad reinsertion can be found in the chapter entitled *Seeking Revenue beyond Advertising*.

6.5 Monitoring the Reinserted Content

From time to time a visitor to your site will object to the fact you are backfilling the ad space, no matter the relevance of the content. If the reinserted ad space becomes empty once again when using an ad blocker it is most likely that the <div> tag has been added to the ad blocker's blacklist. The most widely used list is EasyList which can be reviewed at the following URL:

https://easylist-downloads.adblockplus.org/easylist.txt

Assuming that the tag you are using is named "mybackfill" and that your website domain name is mycompany.com, the entry into the EasyList blacklist will read as follows:

```
mycompany.com###mybackfill
```

If you find an entry in a blacklist, simply modify the <div> tag name within your web pages and the reinserted content will once again appear when an ad blocker is detected.

6.6 Summary

Just because an ad blocker has denied access to an ad server does not mean that the space once occupied by the blocked ad is no longer available to display other content. Ad reinsertion is a technique that allows alternate content to be displayed in place of blocked ads in the form of a request to turn off advertising, a house ad for a relevant product, service or sponsor, or even a donation request.

Chapter 7

7. Using JavaScript Obfuscation

In the same way that visitors to a website can view the HTML used to construct a page by selecting a view source option within the browser window, it is also possible to view the JavaScript code embedded within a page. To avoid this, the JavaScript code should be obfuscated.

In this chapter we will explore the concept of JavaScript obfuscation and the ways in which it can be used as part of an overall strategy to deal with ad blocking.

7.1 What is JavaScript Obfuscation?

The JavaScript contained within a web page is viewable to any visitor that decides to look for it. Even when the JavaScript is contained within a *.js* file that is imported into a web page, that file can be downloaded and viewed at will.

JavaScript obfuscation refers to a technique that is commonly used to obscure the operation and intent of JavaScript code contained within a web page. Consider, for example, the JavaScript detection code introduced in the *Basic Ad Blocker Detection* chapter of this book:

```
(function() {

    var detector = function() {
        setTimeout(function() {

            if(!document.getElementsByClassName) return;
            var ads =
                document.getElementsByClassName('banner_ad'),
            ad  = ads[ads.length - 1];

            if(!ad || ad.innerHTML.length == 0
                    || ad.clientHeight === 0) {
                console.log('Ad Blocker Detected');
            } else {
                console.log('No Ad Blocker');
```

Using JavaScript Obfuscation

```
                }
        }, 2000);
    }

    /* Add a page load listener */
    if(window.addEventListener) {
        window.addEventListener('load', detector, false);
    }
})();
```

It will be clear to anyone with moderate JavaScript skills that the above code is performing some form of ad blocker detection. Consider, however, the same code after it has been obfuscated:

```
var
_0x65ff=["\x67\x65\x74\x45\x6C\x65\x6D\x65\x6E\x74\x73\x42\x79\x43\x6
C\x61\x73\x73\x4E\x61\x6D\x65","\x62\x61\x6E\x6E\x65\x72\x5F\x61\x64"
,"\x6C\x65\x6E\x67\x74\x68","\x69\x6E\x6E\x65\x72\x48\x54\x4D\x4C","\
x63\x6C\x69\x65\x6E\x74\x48\x65\x69\x67\x68\x74","\x41\x64\x20\x42\x6
C\x6F\x63\x6B\x65\x72\x20\x44\x65\x74\x65\x63\x74\x65\x64","\x6C\x6F\
x67","\x4E\x6F\x20\x41\x64\x20\x42\x6C\x6F\x63\x6B\x65\x72","\x61\x64
\x64\x45\x76\x65\x6E\x74\x4C\x69\x73\x74\x65\x6E\x65\x72","\x6C\x6F\x
61\x64"];(function(){var
_0x64b7x1=function(){setTimeout(function(){if(!document[_0x65ff[0]]){
return};var
_0x64b7x2=document[_0x65ff[0]](_0x65ff[1]),_0x64b7x3=_0x64b7x2[_0x64b
7x2[_0x65ff[2]]-
1];if(!_0x64b7x3||_0x64b7x3[_0x65ff[3]][_0x65ff[2]]==0||_0x64b7x3[_0x
65ff[4]]===0){console[_0x65ff[6]](_0x65ff[5])}else
{console[_0x65ff[6]](_0x65ff[7])}},2000)};if(window[_0x65ff[8]]){wind
ow[_0x65ff[8]](_0x65ff[9],_0x64b7x1,false)}})()
```

Clearly it is very difficult to decipher the purpose of the code once it has been obfuscated. The most that can be inferred from the code now is that it checks some aspect of the document and outputs something to the JavaScript console.

7.2 How JavaScript Obfuscation Works

JavaScript is obfuscated by passing the original code through an obfuscator which outputs the obfuscated equivalent code which can then be embedded into a web page. JavaScript obfuscation techniques vary from one obfuscator to another but generally perform the following steps:

1. Rename variables to short meaningless names.

2. Remove unnecessary whitespace and line breaks.
3. Make parts of the code self-generating so that the first execution generates the actual code which is then executed to perform the intended task.
4. Use character codes and string manipulation along with the *eval* function to construct the real JavaScript code.

7.3 JavaScript Obfuscation vs. Minifying

It is important to note that JavaScript obfuscation should not be confused with minified or compressed JavaScript. JavaScript compression is the process of reducing the size of JavaScript code so that it downloads faster when a web page loads. In general terms, steps 1 and 2 outlined above are performed when JavaScript is minified. The following code, for example, lists the same ad blocker detection code after it has been minified:

```
!function(){var
e=function(){setTimeout(function(){if(document.getElementsByClassName
){var e=document.getElementsByClassName("banner_ad"),n=e[e.length-
1];n&&0!=n.innerHTML.length&&0!==n.clientHeight?console.log("No Ad
Blocker"):console.log("Ad Blocker
Detected")}},2e3)};window.addEventListener&&window.addEventListener("
load",e,!1)}();
```

Although the JavaScript code now takes up less space, the intent and purpose of the code is still clear without the additional obfuscation steps.

7.4 JavaScript Obfuscation and Ad Blocking

When taking steps to address ad blocking behavior it is important, even when taking passive steps, to perform these tasks as discretely as possible. This is of particular importance when using strategies such as ad reinsertion as outlined in the previous chapter. When it comes to addressing ad blocking, the less the outside world knows about your activities the better, and JavaScript obfuscation is a useful tool in this context.

One potential problem with using code obfuscation is that some malware detectors will flag a warning when a user loads a web page containing obfuscated code. This is not, however, a common occurrence, nor does it mean the code is necessarily malicious. Rather, it simply means the code is so well obfuscated that the malware detector cannot ascertain what the code actually does.

Using JavaScript Obfuscation

7.5 How to Obfuscate JavaScript Code

An internet search will list a number of free online JavaScript obfuscators, any of which can be used to effectively obfuscate your JavaScript code. One widely used service worth exploring is called JavaScript Obfuscator and is available online at *https://javascriptobfuscator.com*.

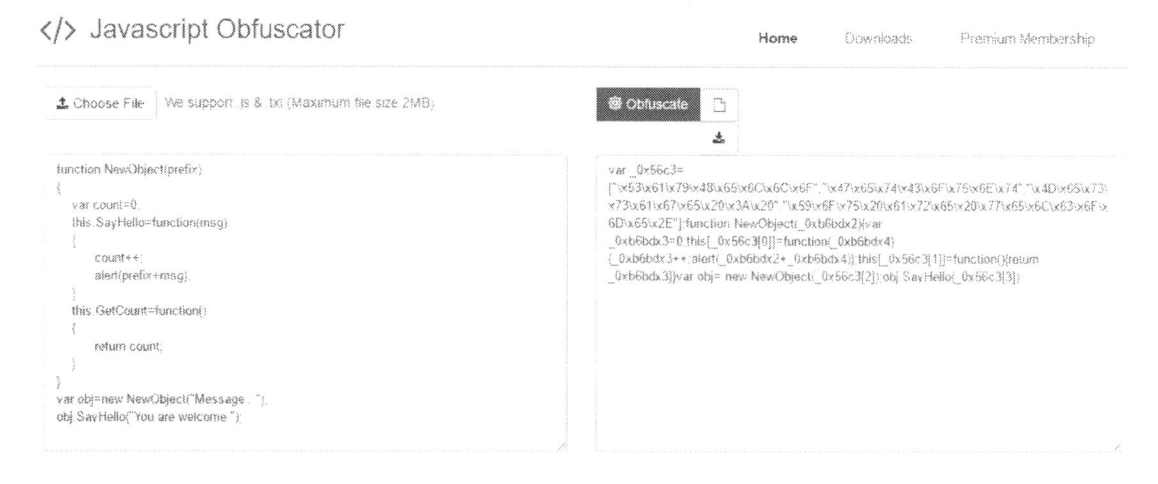

Figure 7-1

Most of these services allow you to paste your JavaScript code into a window and then perform the obfuscation by clicking on a button.

7.6 Summary

Just as visitors to a website can view the HTML used to construct a page by selecting a view source option within the browser window, it is also possible to view the JavaScript code embedded within a website. The term JavaScript obfuscation refers to the process of obscuring the intent and purpose of JavaScript code within a web page, a technique that can be of particular use when taking steps to address ad blocking, particularly when adopting strategies such as ad reinsertion. JavaScript code can be obfuscated using any one of a number of free services provided online.

8. Seeking Revenue beyond Advertising

Part of the process of adapting to the increasingly widespread use of ad blocking involves finding alternative ways to make money from your web traffic. Even if ad blocking is not yet an issue for your website, it still makes sense to transition away from an overdependence on advertising and to generate a more diverse range of revenue streams from your website traffic.

It is all too easy to fall into the trap of equating the level of advertising revenue with the value of the traffic on your website. Publishers of new websites expend vast amounts of effort in search engine optimization in an effort to attract visitors. If you already have a respectable level of traffic to your website you have a valuable asset that can be leverage beyond solely making advertising revenue.

The purpose of this chapter is to outline some suggestions for other ways to find the value in your website traffic. The chapter is not intended to provide an extensive list of options, but rather to outline some strategies that have been proven to work, while providing the inspiration to think beyond advertising as the only source of revenue.

8.1 Sell Digital Goods

Although the size of the online advertising market is impressive it is tiny compared to the size of the market for products and services. Consider, for example, that the value of goods sold by companies in the U.S. alone is measured in trillions of dollars. If you have not considered selling products on your site it is possible you are missing a significant opportunity.

The items that you decide to sell on your site do not have to be physical products. If you operate a website the chances are good that you know a great deal about the subject matter that attracts visitors. Consider writing an eBook on a subject of interest to your visitors and selling copies of it on your website. Once the eBook is written, the margin on each sale is close to 100% percent. A number of digital goods ecommerce services are available (e-junkie.com and payloadz.com being two examples) for selling digital goods for download, allowing you to sell items with little more than a product description and a purchase button.

If the prospect of writing an entire book seems too ambitious, consider creating mini-guides that can be purchased and downloaded. When you have written 10 or 15 mini-guides, bundle them together to create a full book.

A variety of tools are available that will convert your book from the original format (for example Microsoft Word) to PDF, MOBI (Kindle) and ePub (iPad) formats.

If you are able to write a book, consider posting a selection of chapters from the book on your site and encourage visitors to purchase the book to get the remaining chapters.

In addition to selling your eBook direct from your own website, you can also sell it through channels such as Amazon, Apple's iBookStore and Google Play. Though the margins will be smaller, the volumes have the potential to be significantly higher. This particular channel is completely immune to declines in traffic to your website or the effects of ad blocking.

Digital items are not limited to eBooks. Also consider selling shorter documents and access to video streams and webinars.

8.2 Sell Physical Merchandise

These days you don't need an entire manufacturing supply chain to create, sell and deliver physical products. A wide range of merchandise, from print books to iPhone cases can now be created on demand and shipped to customers on your behalf. If you have written an eBook as suggested above, use a print-on-demand service such as Lulu or CreateSpace to get your book in print and sell copies on your website (and through Amazon, book stores etc).

Consider designing a range of products that appeal to your visitor demographic (T-shirts, mouse mats, jackets, coffee cups, beer glasses to name just a few possibilities) and sell them on your web site. If you lack the design skills, decide what you want and use one of the many crowd sourced design services (for example, DesignCrowd and CrowdSpring) to engage the skills of multiple designers. For product ideas, review the range of product options offered by companies such as Teespring, SpreadShirt and CafePress.

8.3 Make Donation Requests

An often overlooked option is to simply ask your visitors to make a donation (in an interesting case of irony, many of the ad blockers on the market are funded entirely through donations from satisfied users).

A request for donations can be made to every visitor, or presented using ad reinsertion so that only visitors with ad blocking enabled see the request. Depending on the wording of the request, some people may donate and others may even choose to turn off their ad blocker when they realize how the website is funded.

The level of donations you receive will likely be greater if you have a loyal base of repeat visitors. Little effort is required, however, to implement donation handling using services such as PayPal as outlined on the following web page:

https://www.paypal.com/webapps/mpp/get-started/donate-button

8.4 Build a Mailing List

A clean and targeted email list is also a valuable asset for a web publisher. It is not uncommon when visiting websites these days for a dialog to appear within a few seconds of landing on the first page asking you to join a mailing list to qualify for a discount or receive a newsletter (and people thought banner ads were annoying). The reason for the popularity of this approach is that mailing lists are a valuable tool for reaching out to your audience. Once you have a mailing list you can use one of the many email marketing services such as ConstantContact, iContact or MailChimp to send regular newsletters to site visitors who have opted-in to your list. These emails can be used extremely cost effectively to drive traffic to your site and to promote and sell more of the products and services you have created.

8.5 Targeting your Email List with Facebook Advertising

Once you have a list of email addresses, that list can then be used to target those people via Facebook advertising. Using the Facebook Ad Manager, you can create a custom audience based on the email addresses in your list. Facebook will then match those email addresses with the email addresses of Facebook profiles and build a custom target audience. This audience may then be further refined based on demographic data such as gender, age and geographical location and used as the basis for advertising campaigns to promote products and services, or simply to drive visitors back to your website.

8.6 Targeting your Audience with the Facebook Pixel

Facebook now has 1.6 billion members. Imagine if you could place an ad within the Facebook news feed of every person who has visited a specific page or group of pages on your website without needing any information about those people. This is achieved by placing a Facebook Pixel (essentially a snippet of JavaScript code) on every page of your website. Over time, this code will build a database of visitors to your site and match them with Facebook profiles. When the time comes to promote your website, product or service, a custom audience can be built from the database. This can be based on a range of options including your entire website traffic, only those Facebook users who visited specific pages, or even users who have not visited your website in a specified amount of time.

Obviously, Facebook does not begin building the visitor database until the pixel code is active on your site. To obtain the Pixel code, begin by going to the following URL, click on *Create Ad* and then, from the initial ad creation screen, select the *Help -> Manage Ads* menu option to access the Ad Manager.

https://www.facebook.com/business/

From within the Ad Manager, select the *Tools -> Pixels* menu option as illustrated in Figure 8-1:

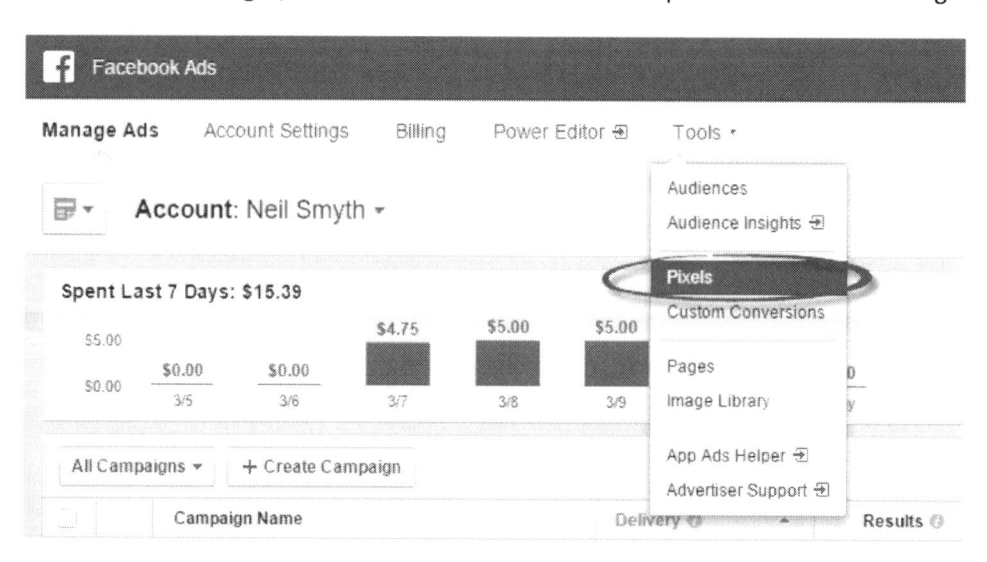

Figure 8-1

On the resulting Pixels panel, enter a name for your pixel and click on the *Create a Pixel* button. Once the pixel code has been generated, add it to the pages of your website. On returning to the Pixels section of the Facebook Ads Manager, data on visitors to your site will be displayed:

Seeking Revenue beyond Advertising

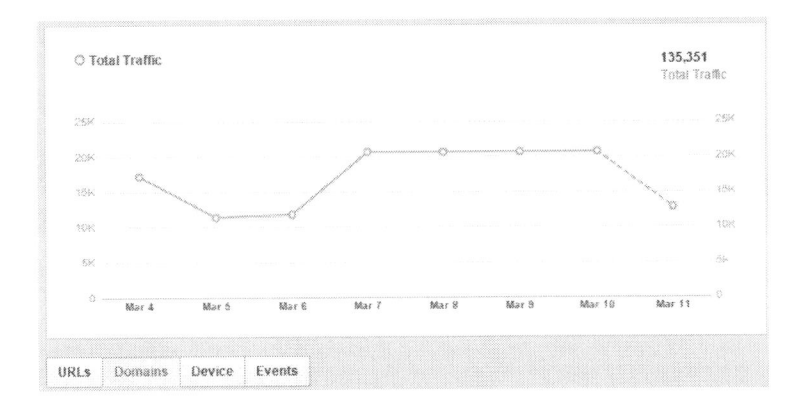

Figure 8-2

The row of options beneath the graph allows statistics to be viewed based on specific web pages, the entire website, device usage and any custom event you may have set up (for example you may have configured the pixel to track every visitor that purchases an eBook or signs up for a newsletter while visiting your site).

To run an advertising campaign targeting visitors to your website simply click on the *Create Custom Audience* button and make the appropriate selections from the resulting panel:

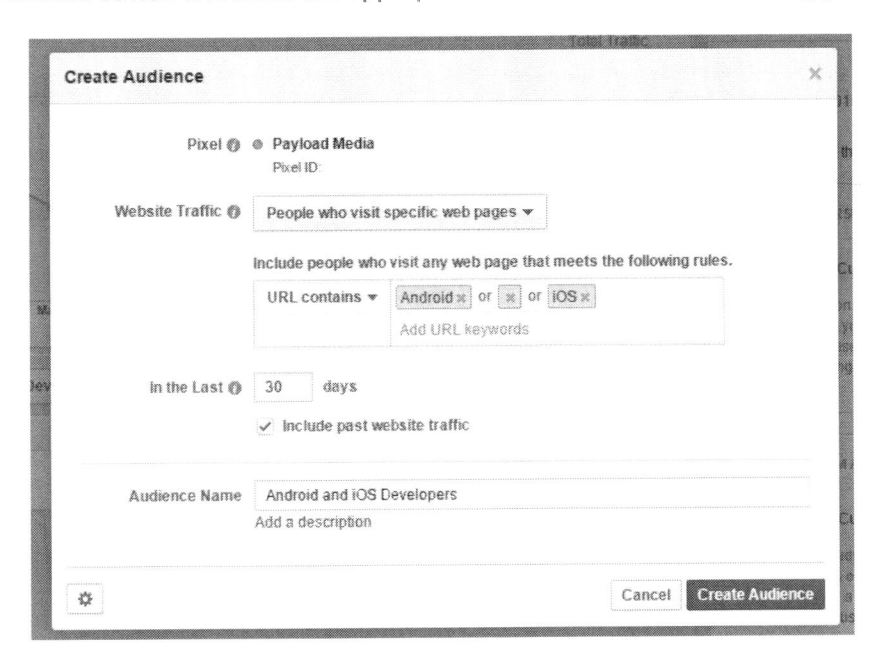

Figure 8-3

Once the custom audience has been saved, it can be used to run a Facebook ad campaign.

55

8.7 Charge for Premium Content

During the Q&A session at a seminar a few years ago the speaker, a successful internet entrepreneur, was asked by an audience member how he made money. His response, much to the amusement of the audience, was that his businesses generated money by asking people to pay for things. In the physical world, the idea of paying for something is hardly a radical business strategy. Unfortunately, internet users have been conditioned to expect (and web publishers resigned to the fact) that content should be given away for free. If the adoption rate of ad blocking continues at the current growth rate, however, there will need to be a change in these expectations. If people do not want to see advertising they will increasingly be required to pay for content.

Setting up a paywall that forces all visitors to pay for content is not the right answer unless you have unique content that cannot be found elsewhere. A more measured approach might be to designate certain areas of your website as being "premium" and charging for access. This might be in the form of content, forums where visitors can ask questions or access to the missing chapters of an eBook that you have only partially published on your website.

If you do not have the time or resources to implement premium content management, a number of third party solutions are available such as those offered by Paywall.com, SubscriptionGenius.com, CoinTent.com and PigeonPaywall.com. For WordPress based sites, the Leaky Paywall plugin is also an option worth consideration.

8.8 Charge Visitors for an Ad Free Experience

Clearly it is possible to detect when a visitor to a website is using an ad blocker. Another potential source of revenue, therefore, is to offer those visitors an ad free experience in return for making either a nominal one time donation, or a periodical subscription payment. A solution similar to this can be integrated using third-party services such as those offered by AdSorcery, details of which are outlined in the chapter entitled *An Overview of BlockAdBlock, AdSorcery and AdBlock X*.

8.9 Sell Advertising and Sponsorship Direct

An interesting option to get around ad blocking is to sell your advertising inventory direct to companies instead of going through third-party ad networks. The key advantages to direct advertising sales is that the ads can be served direct from your website (so will not be blocked by ad blockers) and revenue does not have to be shared with an ad network. As with ad reinsertion, the element containing the ad may get added to an ad blocker list but with careful monitoring this can be resolved simply by renaming the element.

Begin by creating a media kit for your web site (using those provided by other publishers as a template if necessary) and start running ads on your site seeking direct advertisers, even using ad reinsertion to make use of ad inventory lost to ad blocking. Also consider running Google AdWords campaigns using appropriate keywords to gain the attention of potential advertisers.

8.10 Expand Beyond the Website

While ad blocking has the ability to remove ads from a website, no such capability exists for ads that appear in mobile apps. If you have a loyal visitor base that returns frequently to view updated content, it may be worth developing Android and iOS apps to accompany your website and running mobile advertising through the app.

While mobile apps have the advantage of being immune to ad blocking this strategy is not without potential risks. Primarily, mobile apps can be expensive to develop so you will need to be sure that you will get a return on your upfront investment. Also, advertising revenue from mobile apps can be considerably lower than from a website. There is a danger, therefore, that a mobile app may cannibalize your high revenue generating web site traffic and replace it with lower revenue generating mobile app users.

8.11 Summary

While online advertising will continue to be a major source of income for web publishers it should only be part of a diverse range of revenue streams. This chapter has provided some examples of alternate options that can be used to transform web traffic into revenue, many of which will not be impacted by the use of ad blocking.

9. Asking Visitors to Turn Off Ad Blocking

The use of ad blocking has increased over the last few years because many people are tired of visiting websites that are overloaded with intrusive ads. Surveys suggest, however, that many people using ad blockers do not object to advertising appearing on websites as long as those ads do not adversely affect the web browsing experience. The problem for web publishers is that ad blocking technology does not distinguish between websites that use advertising responsibly and those that do not.

In the chapter entitled *Denying Website Access to Ad Blocking Visitors*, we will look at ways to prevent visitors to your site accessing page content until ad blocking is turned off. A more subtle, and often overlooked strategy for dealing with ad blocking, however, is simply to appeal to the better nature of your website visitors by politely asking them to disable ad blocking. In this chapter we will explore some of the ways to go about implementing such a strategy.

9.1 Asking Politely

The objective here is to persuade visitors to turn off ad blocking. This approach will be most successful with regular visitors to your site who appreciate the content that you provide and will be more inclined to respond to a polite request to help keep the website funded. The message should be courteous and explain why the request is being made. The request can be presented in a variety of ways, such as in the form of a notification bar that appears along the top edge of the page, or as a dialog that appears over the top of the content.

When making such a request it is important to achieve the right balance. The idea is not to antagonize visitors to your site, but rather to remind them how much they value your content. If a dialog is used to make the request, visitors should be able to dismiss the dialog and continue accessing the site content (denying access to visitors until ad blocking is disabled is covered in a later chapter). It will also be important to decide whether you want the visitor to see the request on every page visited, or only on the initial landing page.

If your site content targets less technically skilled visitors it may make sense to include a link to a page where steps are provided for whitelisting your website.

9.2 Revising Ad Quality, Quantity and Placement

It is important to keep in mind when asking visitors to disable ad blocking for your website that those visitors can just as easily turn it back on. Before implementing this approach, it is worth taking some time to review the advertising on your website. If your site contains intrusive or excessive advertising, the chances are good that visitors will simply re-enable ad blocking and little will have been gained. Consider reducing the number of ads displayed per page or, as outlined in the next chapter, offering a reduced number of ads in return for disabling ad blocking.

Also experiment with moving any ads located in the main body of your content to the sides of the page (this is particularly worthwhile for CPM-based ads). In general, try to view your site from the point of view of a visitor who has just disabled ad blocking and try to get a sense of whether the experience offered by your site is likely to be tolerable to such visitors.

9.3 The EasyList Adblock Warning Removal List

Many of the techniques outlined in this book are referred to as "anti-ad blocking". Certain types of anti-ad blocking activities are tolerated by keepers of the filter lists used by the ad blockers. The EasyList policy on anti-ad blocking, for example, is available at the following URL:

https://easylist.adblockplus.org/blog/2013/05/10/anti-adblock-guide-for-site-admins

In summary, the policy of this particular list provides very little opportunity to counter ad blocking beyond a polite request that fits into the space and style guidelines provided. The policy implies repercussions for sites that take a more aggressive and intrusive approach. As far as AdBlock Plus and EasyList are concerned, this involves the addition of your site and details of the offending web page element being added to the *EasyList Adblock Warning Removal List*, the content of which can be viewed online at the following URL:

https://easylist-downloads.adblockplus.org/antiadblockfilters.txt

By default, AdBlock Plus does not use this list to block content on websites and must, instead, be manually enabled by users to become effective. As with ad reinsertion, inclusion within the list can often be bypassed by changing the name assigned to the element displaying the ad blocker removal request. Consider, for example, The Atlantic web site, the following entry for which appears in the EasyList warning removal list as follows:

```
theatlantic.com##.blocker-message > .blackbox
```

Read an article on *www.theatlantic.com* with the *EasyList Adblock Warning Removal List* option enabled in the AdBlock Plus settings, however, and the ad blocker removal request is clearly still visible on the web page. A review of the page source reveals that the *blocker-message* name listed in the removal list was simply changed to *blocker-msg* to avoid the removal.

Although there are ways to get around the issue of the EasyList warning removal list, it is important to try to avoid drawing the attention of list maintainers wherever possible. Start out with the least intrusive approach to asking visitors to disable ad blocking for your site, graduating to the more intrusive options when you begin to feel you have little to lose by becoming more aggressive.

9.4 Displaying a Notification Bar

A notification bar is a less intrusive option and is recommended as the first step in implementing this strategy. The notification takes the form of a bar that appears across the top or bottom edge of the page when a visitor has an ad blocker enabled (Figure 9-1 illustrates a notification bar attached to the top edge of the browser window). The notification bar can be configured to remain fixed and continuously visible, or allowed to scroll out of view along with the content of the web page. An optional close button may be included to allow the site visitor to dismiss the bar from view:

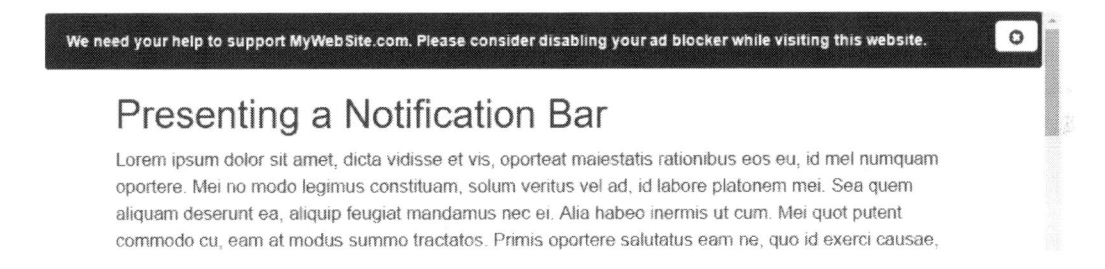

Figure 9-1

Though a variety of techniques are available for displaying a notification bar within a web page, this chapter will make use of the NavBar component from the Bootstrap JavaScript framework. This component provides a range of configuration options including positioning the bar at the top or bottom of the page, and the ability to fix the bar so that it remains visible during page scrolling.

This chapter assumes the implementation of some form of ad blocker detection such as those outlined in the chapter entitled *Basic Ad Blocker Detection*. The use of the Bootstrap framework

Asking Visitors to Turn Off Ad Blocking

requires that some items be imported into the web pages on which the notification is to appear, for example:

```html
<html>
<head>
<script src=
 "https://ajax.googleapis.com/ajax/libs/jquery/1.12.0/jquery.min.js">
</script>
<script src=
"http://maxcdn.bootstrapcdn.com/bootstrap/3.3.6/js/bootstrap.min.js">
</script>
<link rel="stylesheet" href=
"http://maxcdn.bootstrapcdn.com/bootstrap/3.3.6/css/bootstrap.min.css
">
</head>
```

Next, some CSS styles need to be declared to customize the appearance of the notification bar. The following style directives specify background and text colors:

```html
<style>
.navbar-custom {
    background-color: blue;
}

.navbar-text {
        color: white !important;
}

.navbar-header{
  margin-left:5px;
  width:99%;
}
</style>
```

Finally, the following code should be placed within the section of the detection code that is executed when an ad blocker is detected:

```
$('body').prepend('<div id="notify" \
  class="navbar navbar-default navbar-custom "> \
   <div class="navbar-header navbar-custom"> \
    <p class="navbar-text"><b>We need your help to support \
    MyWebSite.com. Please consider disabling your ad blocker.<b></p> \
   </div> \
```

Asking Visitors to Turn Off Ad Blocking

```
</div> ');
```

When the above code is executed the notification will appear along the top edge of the browser window and will scroll out of view as the page content scrolls.

To fix the notification so that it remains locked in position at the top of the page, simply add the *navbar-fixed-top* class to the element:

```
$('body').prepend('<div id="notify" \
   class="navbar navbar-default navbar-custom navbar-fixed-top"> \
  <div class="navbar-header navbar-custom"> \
   <p class="navbar-text"><b>We need your help to support \
         MyWebSite.com. Please consider disabling your ad blocker.<b></p> \
  </div> \
</div> ');
```

Move the bar to the bottom of the page using the *navbar-fixed-bottom* option:

```
$('body').prepend('<div id="notify" \
   class="navbar navbar-default navbar-custom navbar-fixed-bottom"> \
  <div class="navbar-header navbar-custom"> \
   <p class="navbar-text"><b>We need your help to support \
         MyWebSite.com. Please consider disabling your ad blocker.<b></p> \
  </div> \
</div> ');
```

Finally, the following changes will add a button which, when clicked, will dismiss the notification:

```
$('body').prepend('<div id="notify" \
   class="navbar navbar-default navbar-custom navbar-fixed-top"> \
  <div class="navbar-header navbar-custom"> \
   <p class="navbar-text"><b>We need your help to support \
    MyWebSite.com. Please consider disabling your ad blocker.<b></p> \
   <button type="button" id="close-btn" \
       class="btn btn-default navbar-btn pull-right"> \
     <span class="glyphicon glyphicon-remove-sign" \
           aria-hidden="true"></span> \
   </button> \
  </div> \
</div> ');
```

Asking Visitors to Turn Off Ad Blocking

```
$("#close-btn").click(function(){
     $("#notify").hide();
});
```

Visit the following URL to see a notification bar example in action:

See it in Action

http://www.techotopia.com/survival/navbar.html

9.5 Displaying a Dialog Request

Displaying the request within a dialog is a somewhat more invasive approach. The dialog is displayed when the detection code identifies the presence of an ad blocker and typically involves the content of the web page appearing with a dark overlay while the dialog is displayed (Figure 9-2). When using a dialog, the visitor should be able to easily dismiss the dialog by clicking a button.

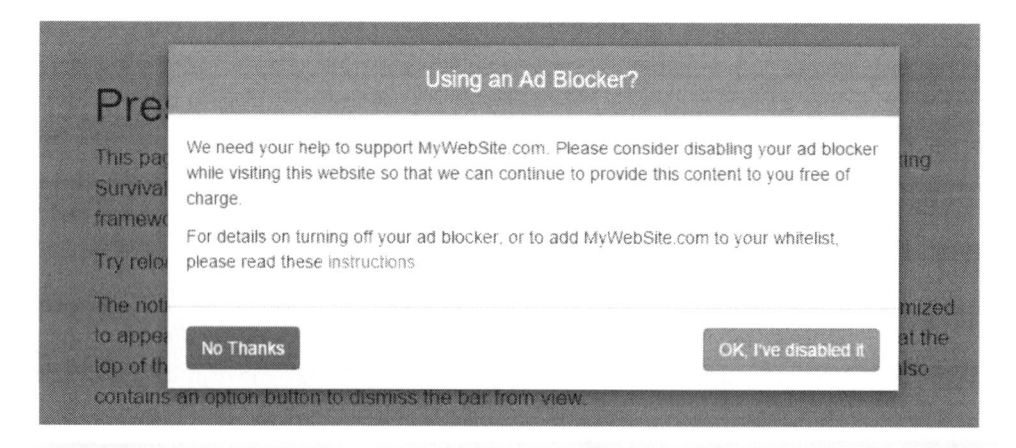

Figure 9-2

For the purposes of this chapter, an example request dialog will be implemented using the Bootstrap framework Modal Plugin. As with the NavBar example, the use of the Bootstrap framework requires that some items be imported into the web pages on which the dialog is to appear, for example:

```
<html>
<head>
<script src=
 "https://ajax.googleapis.com/ajax/libs/jquery/1.12.0/jquery.min.js">
</script>
```

Asking Visitors to Turn Off Ad Blocking

```
<script src=
"http://maxcdn.bootstrapcdn.com/bootstrap/3.3.6/js/bootstrap.min.js">
</script>
<link rel="stylesheet" href=
"http://maxcdn.bootstrapcdn.com/bootstrap/3.3.6/css/bootstrap.min.css
">
</head>
```

By default, the modal dialog appears with a white background. To add some color to the dialog some additional CSS styles may be declared. The following example configures the dialog to appear with a green header displaying white text and the footer shaded gray:

```
<style>

   .modal-header, h4, .close {
      background-color: #5cb85c;
      color:white !important;
      text-align: center;
   }

   .modal-body {
   }

   .modal-footer {
      background-color: #f9f9f9;
   }
</style>
```

The modal dialog and corresponding content are declared within the web page as follows:

```
<div class="modal fade" id="myModal" role="dialog"
                                 data-backdrop="static">
  <div class="modal-dialog">

    <!-- Modal content-->
    <div class="modal-content">
      <div class="modal-header">
        <h4 class="modal-title">Using an Ad Blocker?</h4>
      </div>
      <div class="modal-body">
        <p>We need your help to support MyWebSite.com. Please
consider disabling your ad blocker while visiting this website so
```

Asking Visitors to Turn Off Ad Blocking

```
that we can continue to provide this content to you free of
charge.</p>
        <p>For details on turning off your ad blocker, or to add
MyWebSite.com to your whitelist, please read these
<a href="#">instructions</a></p>
      </div>
      <div class="modal-footer">
        <button type="button" id="no-button"
             class="btn btn-primary pull-left" >No Thanks</button>
        <button type="button" id="ok-button"
             class="btn btn-success" >OK, I've disabled it</button>
      </div>
    </div>

  </div>
</div>
```

The above HTML represents the dialog shown in Figure 9-2 and may, of course, be customized to display different text. Note that the footer section of the dialog contains two buttons. The first displays a "No Thanks" message and will be configured to close the dialog. The second button displays text which reads "OK, I've disabled it". This button will be configured such that if the user clicks on it to indicate that ad blocking has been disabled, the page will reload so that the ads become visible.

By default, the Bootstrap Modal dialog can be dismissed by clicking anywhere within the page content. Since we want the user to click on one of the two buttons to dismiss the dialog this default behavior has been disabled by setting the "backdrop" property to "static":

```
<div class="modal fade" id="myModal"
                    role="dialog" data-backdrop="static">
```

When an ad blocker is detected, the above dialog can be displayed using the following code:

```
$("#myModal").modal("show");
```

When the user dismisses the dialog, it can be hidden as follows:

```
$("#myModal").hide();
```

9.6 Showing the Dialog and Responding to Button Clicks

With the dialog designed and implemented, the standard ad blocker detection code can be extended to display the dialog and to configure click event handlers for the two buttons. Assuming the standard detection code, this can be implemented as follows:

```
.
.
.
var detector = function() {
    setTimeout(function() {

        if(!document.getElementsByClassName) return;
        var ads = document.getElementsByClassName('banner_ad'),
            ad  = ads[ads.length - 1];

        if(!ad || ad.innerHTML.length == 0
                    || ad.clientHeight === 0) {
            $("#myModal").modal("show");
            $("#no-button").click(function(){
                $("#myModal").modal("hide");
            });

            $("#ok-button").click(function(){
                window.location.reload();
            });
        }

    }, 2000);
}
.
.
.
```

When an ad blocker is detected, the modal dialog is displayed. Actions are then assigned to the two buttons. The button designated as *no-button* hides the dialog while *ok-button* reloads the web page so that the ads will appear.

Visit the following web page to see an example of the Bootstrap Modal Plugin working in conjunction with ad blocker detection code:

Asking Visitors to Turn Off Ad Blocking

See it in Action

http://www.techotopia.com/survival/dialog.html

9.7 Adding Tracking Code

Data about the number of visitors who opt to disable ad blocking in response to the request can be tracked using the techniques outlined in the chapter entitled *Assessing the Damage*. Assuming that you have a Google Analytics account and the tracking code embedded in your web pages, tracking can be implemented by sending different events depending on the dialog button selection made by the visitor:

```
if(!ad || ad.innerHTML.length == 0
           || ad.clientHeight === 0) {
    $("#myModal").modal("show");
    $("#no-button").click(function(){
        $("#myModal").modal("hide");
        ga('send', {
            'hitType': 'event',
            'eventCategory': 'DisabledAdblocker',
            'eventAction': 'Not Disabled',
            'nonInteraction': 1
        });
    });

    $("#ok-button").click(function(){
        $("#myModal").hide();
        ga('send', {
            'hitType': 'event',
            'eventCategory': 'DisabledAdblocker',
            'eventAction': 'Disabled',
            'nonInteraction': 1
        });
        window.location.reload();
    });
}
```

9.8 Implementing a Timeout Delay

After a while running a campaign to persuade site visitors to disable ad blocking, the data gathered may suggest that most visitors aren't being persuaded, even if the request appears on every page that they visit. A slight adjustment to this strategy is to continue to allow the dialog to be dismissed instantly if the visitor disables ad blocking, but to introduce a delay before the dialog can be dismissed if ad blocking remains enabled.

The final task in this chapter is to make some changes to the detection code used previously so that the "No Thanks" button is disabled until a timeout period has elapsed. The button will display a countdown of the remaining seconds and will be enabled when the count reaches zero:

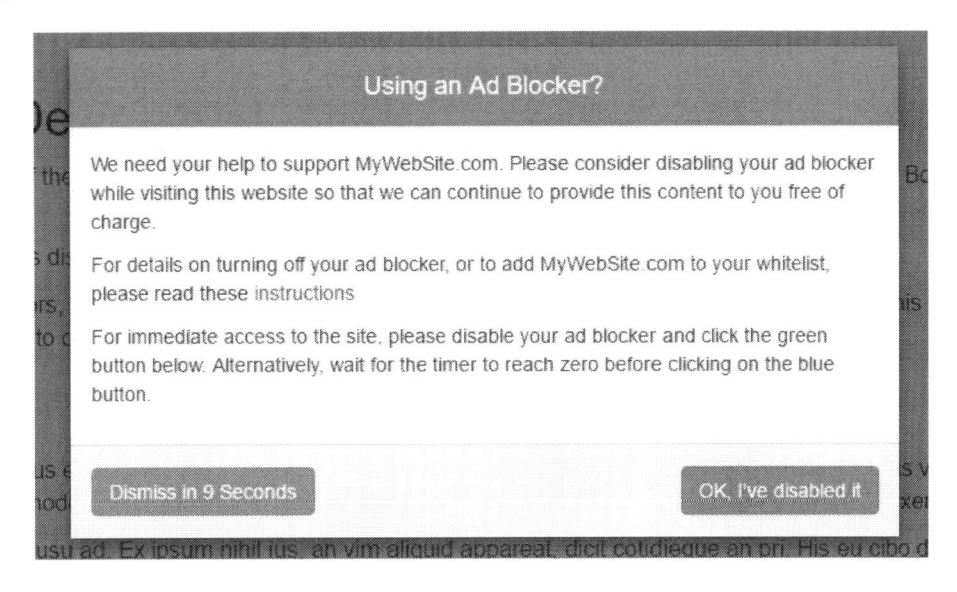

Figure 9-3

Begin by editing the ad blocker detection code to implement a new JavaScript function named *buttonDelay* which takes as an argument a timeout value in seconds:

```
<div class="banner_ad"> </div>
<script>

function buttonDelay(secs) {

    if(secs < 1) {
        clearTimeout(timer);
        $("#no-button").prop('disabled', false);
        $("#no-button").text('Dismiss');
        $("#no-button").click(function(){
            $("#myModal").modal("hide");
        });
    } else {
        secs--;
        $("#no-button").text('Dismiss in ' + secs + ' seconds');
```

Asking Visitors to Turn Off Ad Blocking

```
            var timer = setTimeout('buttonDelay('+secs+')',1000);
        }
    }

    (function() {

            var detector = function() {
                setTimeout(function() {
.
.
.
```

This function begins by checking whether the number of seconds remaining has reached zero. If it has not yet reach zero, the number of seconds remaining is decreased by one and the text on the button updated with a new text string displaying the new countdown value. A timeout is then configured to wait one second before calling the *buttonDelay()* function once again. This process will repeat until the number of seconds remaining reaches zero.

On reaching zero, the button appearance is changed so that it is no longer grayed out, the text is changed in "Dismiss" and an action assigned so that the button can now be clicked to hide the modal dialog.

All that remains now is to modify the main detector code. This code now needs to set the button as being disabled and call the *buttonDelay()* function passing through the duration of the delay in seconds. Since we do not want the user to be able to dismiss the dialog until the timeout has elapsed, the code to add the hide action to the button must be removed. Once these changes have been made the detection function should read as follows:

```
(function() {

        var detector = function() {
            setTimeout(function() {

                if(!document.getElementsByClassName) return;
                var ads =
                        document.getElementsByClassName('banner_ad'),
                    ad  = ads[ads.length - 1];

                if(!ad || ad.innerHTML.length == 0
                                || ad.clientHeight === 0) {
                    $("#myModal").modal("show");
```

```
                $("#no-button").prop('disabled', true);
                buttonDelay(10);

                $("#no-button").click(function(){
                    $("#myModal").modal("hide");
                });

                $("#ok-button").click(function(){
                    window.location.reload();
                });

            }

        }, 2000);
    }

    /* Add a page load listener */
    if(window.addEventListener) {
        window.addEventListener('load', detector, false);
    }
})();
```

With the above changes complete, the dialog will appear as before when a visitor is using an ad blocker. If the visitor disables the ad blocker and clicks the green button, immediate access to the content is granted. Alternatively, the blue button will count down the number of seconds remaining during which time clicking on the button will have no effect. After the timeout has elapsed, however, the text on the button will change to read "Dismiss" and may be clicked to close the dialog.

To see this code in action go to the following URL:

See it in Action

http://www.techotopia.com/survival/timedialog.html

9.9 Summary

Studies suggest that many people will turn off ad blocking if requested to do so as long as the appearance of advertising does not degrade the user experience. A simple, polite request to turn off ad blocking is arguably the most subtle approach to dealing with ad blocking and may be implemented using ad reinsertion, a notification bar or a modal dialog. The effectiveness of such

Asking Visitors to Turn Off Ad Blocking

a strategy can be tracked using Google Analytics events and modified to introduce a delay for those users unwilling to disable ad blocking on your site.

Chapter 10

10. Controlling Ad Blocker Removal Request Frequency

If you have decided to adopt a strategy aimed at persuading visitors to disable ad blocking on your site, the next step is to decide the frequency with which the request should be presented to each visitor in the event that ad blocking remains enabled.

This chapter will outline some factors to take into consideration when deciding on request frequency before introducing some techniques to implement the functionality.

10.1 Deciding on Request Frequency

The objective of asking visitors to turn off ad blocking is, of course, to persuade as many visitors as possible to do so. If a visitor to your site turns off ad blocking as a result of the request then for that person the objective has been met. The question that needs to be considered is what to do about the visitors that continue to use ad blocking.

Suppose that a visitor with ad blocking enabled lands on your website and is presented with the request dialog or notification bar asking that the ad blocker be disabled. This visitor closes the request and continues to access the content on your site without disabling ad blocking. You have the choice of displaying the request every time the visitor loads another page or returns to your website in the future. Alternatively you might decide to show the request again after the visitor has visited another three pages. Another option is to allow the visitor to continue to access pages for another 24 hours before showing the request again.

The best option will depend to a large extent on the typical behavior of your visitors and how valuable they are to you even with ad blocking enabled. If your site has a high percentage of repeat visitors, for example, then you may want to consider showing them the request once each time they arrive on your site but not on every page they visit. This can be achieved by setting a time duration that must elapse before a visitor sees the reminder again. If, on the other hand, most people visiting your site are doing so for the first time and have a tendency to read more than two pages before leaving, it may make sense to display the message once on the first page and then again when the visitor displays the third or fourth page of content. Some combination of these options is also worth considering.

The risk with displaying the request too frequently is that it may antagonize visitors to the extent that they decide to avoid your website in the future, or go looking for solutions to subvert your ad blocker detection code (using a so-called "anti-ad block killer"). If visitors to your site have no value to you if they are blocking ads then showing the request on every page and every visit may be an appropriate strategy. If your website has other objectives beyond generating advertising revenue (such as selling products or services using house ads or building email address lists) then a more subtle approach is warranted so as not to drive away future traffic.

Clearly the best strategy to adopt will depend on your specific website traffic and visitor behavior. Once the decision has been made, however, the steps to implement the chosen request frequency are relatively easy to implement. Before doing so, however, it is important to understand the concept of browser cookies.

10.2 An Introduction to Cookies

The word *cookie* is one of those technological terms where the name does nothing to convey what the feature actually does. It is commonly believed that even the people at Netscape responsible for devising and implementing cookies didn't really have a valid reason for selecting the name. Questionable naming aside, JavaScript cookies are actually an extremely powerful feature.

10.3 What is a JavaScript Cookie?

Cookies allow a website to store information on the computers of the visitors browsing the website. Cookies hold string based name/value pairs (i.e. *name=value* settings), are limited to a maximum of 4kb in size each, and a single server or website domain can only store a total of 20 cookies per user browser.

Another common limitation of cookies is that browsers can be configured to turn off support for cookies. There is the possibility, therefore, that the frequency tracking code outlined in this chapter will fail to function for a certain percentage of your visitors.

Despite the limitations outlined above, cookies provide an excellent way to maintain state on the client's browser. For example, a cookie can be used to keep count of the number of pages a visitor has loaded, or days that have elapsed since that person was last asked to disable ad blocking.

10.4 The Structure of a Cookie

Cookies are created using the *cookie* property of the *Document* object. The format of a cookie is as follows:

```
name=value; expires=expirationDateGMT; path=URLpath;
domain=siteDomain
```

10.4.1 Cookie Name / Value Pair

The first section of the cookie defines the name of the cookie and the value assigned to the cookie. Both the *name* and *value* settings can be anything you choose to use. For example, you might want to save a user's currency preference - *currency=USDollars*. This is the only section of the cookie that is mandatory. The following settings can be omitted from the cookies if they are not required.

10.4.2 Cookie Expiration Setting

The optional *expires=* section specifies the date on which the cookie should expire. The JavaScript Date object can be used to obtain and manipulate dates for this purpose.

For example, to set a cookie to expire after 6 months have elapsed:

```
var expirationDate = new Date;
expirationDate.setMonth(expirationDate.getMonth()+6)
```

10.4.3 Cookie *path* Setting

The *path=* setting allows a URL to be stored in the cookie. By default, cookies are accessible only to web pages in the same directory as the web page which originally created the cookie. For example, if the cookie was created when the user loaded *http://www.techotopia.com/intro/index.html* that cookie will be accessible to any other pages in the */intro* directory, but not to pages in */navigation*. By specifying *path=/navigation* this limitation is removed.

10.4.4 Cookie *domain* Setting

Similar to the path setting, cookies are only accessible to web pages residing on the server domain from which the cookie was originally created. For example, a cookie created by a web page residing on *www.techotopia.com* is not, by default, accessible to a web page hosted on *www.linuxtopia.org*. Access to the cookie from web pages on linuxtopia.org can be enabled with a *domain=linxutopia.org* setting.

10.5 Configuring Expiration-based Requests

The first example in this chapter will ensure that a request to turn off ad blocking is made to a visitor only once in each 24 hour period. In other words, once a visitor to your site has seen the request once, regardless of how many times they visit in the next 24 hours they will not see the request again. After 24 hours have passed the request will be displayed the next time the visitor arrives, and the cycle will repeat.

The first step is to implement a JavaScript function to detect and retrieve a cookie from the browser:

```
function getCookie(cname) {
    var name = cname + "=";
    var ca = document.cookie.split(';');
    for(var i=0; i<ca.length; i++) {
        var c = ca[i];
        while (c.charAt(0)==' ') c = c.substring(1);
        if (c.indexOf(name) == 0) return
        c.substring(name.length,c.length);
    }
    return "";
}
```

Next, a function needs to be defined for the purpose of writing the cookie to the browser with an expiration date set to a specified number of hours in the future:

```
function setCookie(cname, cvalue, expirationhours) {
    var date = new Date();
    date.setTime(date.getTime() + (expirationhours*60*60*1000));
    var expires = "expires="+date.toUTCString();
    console.log(expires);
    document.cookie = cname + "=" + cvalue + "; " + expires;
}
```

Finally, code is needed to check for the presence of the cookie. If it is not present this is either a new visitor or 24 hours have elapsed since this person was last shown the ad blocker removal request. Either way, the cookie needs to be set again. This is achieved by calling the above *setCookie()* function, passing through the name ("notify"), the value ("true") and the number of hours to expiration (24). Having written the cookie to the browser's cookie storage, the ad blocker request is then displayed:

```
if (getCookie("notified") == "") {
```

```
    // Cookie is not set. Set cookie with 24 hour expiration…
    setCookie("notified", "true", 24);
    // … and display ad blocker request
    $("#myModal").modal("show");
}
```

To see a working example of this technique, visit the following URL. Note that for testing purposes the cookie used in this example is set to expire after one minute:

See it in Action

http://www.techotopia.com/survival/expiration.html

Load the above page into a browser with an ad blocker enabled and wait for the appearance of the request dialog. Immediately reload the page and note that the dialog does not appear. After one minute has elapsed, reload the page a third time, at which point the dialog will reappear.

10.6 Displaying the Request Based on Page Views

The second approach is to keep a count of the number of pages viewed by a visitor, only displaying the request when a specified number of pages have been viewed. While this technique can be combined with a time expiration, for the purposes of this example only the page view count will be used in determining whether a request needs to be displayed.

As is the case with most examples in this book, the following code will need to be executed in the event that the presence of an ad blocker is detected. First, a modified version of the *setCookie()* method that does not set an expiration needs to be implemented:

```
function setCookie(cname, cvalue) {
    document.cookie = cname + "=" + cvalue;
}
```

Next, a new function will be implemented which will be called when an ad blocker is detected and will return a true value if the request needs to be displayed:

```
function checkPageViewCount() {
    var countStr = getCookie("viewcount");
    var countInt;
    var result = false;
    var maxcount = 3;

    if (countStr == "") {
```

Controlling Ad Blocker Removal Request Frequency

```
            result = true;
            countInt = 1;
        } else {
            countInt = parseInt(countStr);
            if (countInt == maxcount) {
                result = true;
                countInt = 1;
            } else {
                countInt++;
            }
        }
        setCookie("viewcount", countInt);
        return result;
}
```

The code begins by attempting to get the cookie from the browser. If the cookie does not exist the result variable is set to *true* and the page view count set to 1.

```
var countStr = getCookie("viewcount");
var countInt;
var result = false;
var maxcount = 3;

if (countStr == "") {
    result = true;
    countInt = 1;
}
```

If the cookie exists, the page count value is converted to an integer (remember that cookies are only able to store string values) and checked to see if it has reached the maximum page views allowed before the request is to be displayed (in this case 3 pages). If this is the third page opened by the site visitor the result value is set to *true* (indicating the request needs to be displayed) and the count reset to 1:

```
else {
    countInt = parseInt(countStr);
    if (countInt == maxcount) {
        result = true;
        countInt = 1;
    }
```

If the page count has not yet reached the maximum allowed page views, the page count is incremented:

```
else {
        countInt++;
}
```

Finally, the current page count value is saved to the cookie and the result variable returned:

```
setCookie("viewcount", countInt);
return result;
```

All that remains is to call the *checkPageViewCount()* function when an ad blocker is detected and display the ad blocker removal request in the event that a *true* result is returned, for example:

```
if (checkPageViewCount() == true) {
    $("#myModal").modal("show");
}
```

To see the above code in action, visit the following web page:

See it in Action

http://www.techotopia.com/survival/pagecount.html

10.7 Offer a Less Ad Intensive Experience

Since visitors have the choice of ignoring the request and continuing on with ad blocking enabled, it may be worth sweetening the request with an offer to reduce the number of ads displayed in return for disabling ad blocking. This can be achieved using the steps outlined in the chapter entitled *Filling Blocked Ads with Ad Reinsertion* to write empty content to the some of your ad elements combined with a cookie to identify visitors entitled to fewer ads when they return to your website in future (assuming of course that they have not re-instated ad blocking on your site in the meantime).

10.8 Summary

When requesting that site visitors whitelist your website, it is important to decide the frequency with which the request should be made in the event that the user continues to block ads. Frequency can be based on the number of page views, elapsed time or a combination of the two. Ad removal requests may also be combined with ad reinsertion to offer visitors less ads in return for whitelisting your site.

Controlling Ad Blocker Removal Request Frequency

As outlined in this chapter, request frequency can be implemented by making use of JavaScript cookies.

11. Denying Website Access to Ad Blocking Visitors

The previous chapters have outlined ways to encourage visitors to either whitelist your website or temporarily disable their ad blocker while reading your site content. By design, this approach allows the visitor to continue accessing your site even if they decline to disable ad blocking. The objective of this approach is to appeal to the better nature of your visitors in the hope that enough of them will accede to the request without antagonizing loyal (albeit ad blocker wielding) visitors.

This chapter will move on to the more aggressive approach of denying website access to any visitors using ad blocking.

11.1 Does this Approach Work?

An interesting survey of ad blocker users in the United Kingdom was performed by the Interactive Advertising Bureau UK (IAB UK). Of those responding to the survey, 54% said they would disable their ad blocker if doing so was the only way to access the content on a website. This percentage rises to 73% for respondents in the 18 to 24 year old age group.

The same survey also found that 20% of ad blocker users indicated that they no longer used ad blocking after being unable to access desired content. It was also found that 64% of ad blocker users in the survey reporting having received a request to disable ad blocking when visiting a website.

It would seem, therefore, that there is both a precedent and a strong case for denying access to visitors using an ad blocker. While certainly a valid strategy for dealing with ad blocking, it is important to make a fully informed decision after also taking into consideration the potential risks of this approach.

11.2 Use with Caution

Denying access to visitors if they have an active ad blocker is probably the most extreme measure available to website publishers and is not an option that should be adopted without due consideration. It is important to remember that ad blocking is growing in popularity for the simple reason that ad blockers improve the web experience for most users. Denying access to your visitors if they are using an ad blocker is likely to annoy many of those visitors. Encountering a barrier that denies access until the ad blocker is disabled may cause the visitor to abandon your site and seek similar content elsewhere. If your site content is unique, there is also the risk that determined, technologically savvy visitors will seek out ways to circumvent your ad blocker detection code.

It is also important to keep in mind that not all ad blocking takes the form of a browser plugin that is under the control of the person visiting your site. Due to the prevalence of malware in advertising code, many corporate firewalls contain built-in ad blocking technology over which the individual employee has little if any control. If the content on your website is particularly relevant to corporate employees while they are at work, there is the real danger that they will be unable to meet the demand that ad blocking be disabled and will be locked out from your site.

It is far better, therefore, to find other ways to mitigate the loss of advertising revenue than to use what might best be described as the "nuclear option" of denying access. That being said, there are still valid reasons for using this option:

- The majority of your website revenue is advertising based, and requesting that visitors disable ad blocking has not made a significant difference.
- All other avenues of generating revenue from your web traffic have failed.
- Only a small proportion of your web traffic comes from corporate visitors.

If, after considering the risks and benefits, you essentially arrive at the conclusion that you have nothing to lose by adopting this strategy then the steps to do so are straightforward.

11.3 Denying Access when Ad Blocking is Enabled

Access denial is best used in conjunction with the dialog request approach outlined in the chapter entitled *Asking Visitors to Turn Off Ad Blocking*. Instead of allowing the visitor to dismiss the dialog and continue accessing the site however, the code will be modified to detect whether the ad blocker has been disabled when the dialog is closed. Assuming the continued use of the Bootstrap Modal plugin to present the dialog, the plugin will be configured such that it calls a

Denying Website Access to Ad Blocking Visitors

function when it is about to close. This function will force the web page to reload which, in turn, will cause the ad blocker detection code to be executed once again. If the ad blocker is still enabled, the dialog will appear. If, on the other hand, the user disabled the ad blocker the code to display the dialog will not execute and the visitor will gain unhindered access to the site content. Since the page reloaded after the ad blocker was disabled, all of the previously blocked ads will once again appear.

To add this functionality to the example created in the *Asking Visitors to Turn Off Ad Blocking* chapter, just two extra lines of code are required:

```
var detector = function() {
    setTimeout(function() {

        if(!document.getElementsByClassName) return;
        var ads =
                document.getElementsByClassName('banner_ad'),
            ad = ads[ads.length - 1];

        if(!ad || ad.innerHTML.length == 0
                    || ad.clientHeight === 0) {
            $("#myModal").modal("show");
            $("#myModal").on('hide.bs.modal', function () {
                window.location.reload();
            });
        }
    }, 2000);
}
```

The additional lines of code configure the Modal dialog to execute a *window.location.reload()* function call when the dialog is about to be hidden (in other words the user has clicked on the close button to dismiss the dialog). When called, *window.location.reload()* function forces the browser to reload the web page.

While the dialog is displayed, the content of the web page will be visible but will appear with a dark overlay. The user will not, however, be able to scroll the page to view more content than is currently visible. If the dialog does not obscure enough of the content, consider increasing the dialog size by adding more content to the message, perhaps explaining why this action has become necessary. The width of the modal dialog may also be increased using the *modal-lg* class when declaring the modal element:

```
<div class="modal fade" id="myModal" role="dialog">
```

```
   <div class="modal-dialog modal-lg">

     <!-- Modal content-->
     <div class="modal-content">
       <div class="modal-header">
.
.
.
</div>
```

Visit the following URL to see this strategy in action:

See it in Action

http://www.techotopia.com/survival/denial.html

11.4 Offer a Less Ad Intensive Experience

As with the ad blocker removal request strategy, consider offering the visitor a browsing experience containing less ads in return for disabling ad blocking while visiting your site. As outlined in the chapter entitled *Controlling Ad Blocker Removal Request Frequency*, this can be achieved using ad reinsertion (as outlined in *Filling Blocked Ads with Ad Reinsertion*) combined with a cookie to allow the agreement to be honored when visitors return to the site in the future.

11.5 Summary

If insufficient users disable ad blocking when asked to do so, another option is to deny access until the visitor complies. Although a valid approach that is gaining in popularity among web publishers, this strategy is not without some risks including alienating loyal visitors and denying access to corporate employees unable to comply with the request to disable ad blocking. As outlined in the next chapter, the success rate of such an approach can and should be monitored carefully.

# Chapter 12

12. Tracking the Visitor Response Rate

When using the access denial strategy outlined in the previous chapter it will be important to track the number of visitors who disabled ad blocking in relation to those that were driven away by the restriction. This will allow you to gauge the effectiveness of this approach over an extended period of time.

This chapter will build on the Google Analytics tracking techniques outlined in the chapter entitled *Assessing the Damage* combined with the use of a cookie to track the effectiveness of the strategy.

12.1 How the Tracking Works

The access denial example covered in the previous chapter detects the presence of an ad blocker and repeatedly displays a dialog until the ad blocker is disabled. In order to track the number of visitors who turned off ad blocking in relation to those who left the site, the following sequence of actions will be taken within the web page code:

A. Detection code identifies the presence of an ad blocker:
   1. Displays a dialog instructing visitor to disable the ad blocker.
   2. Checks to see if a "request made" cookie has already been stored in the user's browser.
   3. If the cookie does not exist, create and store the cookie with a 30 second expiration and send a "request made" event to Google Analytics.

B. Detection code finds no active ad blocker:
   1. Check for existence of "request made" cookie. If it does not exist the visitor landed on the site without an ad blocker enabled. No action necessary.
   2. If the cookie exists, the user has complied with the dialog and turned off the ad blocker. Send "complied" event to Google Analytics.

Tracking the Visitor Response Rate

The above sequence of steps uses the cookie with a 30 second expiration to ensure that only the first attempt by the user to load the web page with an ad blocker enabled is recorded. This is intended to filter out instances whereby a visitor dismisses the dialog multiple times in the hope that it will go away. Google Analytics events are used to keep track of visitors that arrive with ad blocking enabled and those who turn off ad blocking in response to the dialog in order to gain access to the site content.

12.2 Preparing for Tracking Implementation

For the purposes of this chapter, the blocking example created in the previous chapter will be extended to implement the tracking steps outlined above. If your website is not already using Google Analytics, follow the steps in the *Assessing the Damage* chapter of this book to create an account and integrate the code into the pages of your website.

The code will also make use of the *getCookie()* function created in the chapter entitled *Controlling Ad Blocker Removal Request Frequency*. This function reads as follows:

```
<script>
function getCookie(cname) {
    var name = cname + "=";
    var ca = document.cookie.split(';');
    for(var i=0; i<ca.length; i++) {
        var c = ca[i];
        while (c.charAt(0)==' ') c = c.substring(1);
        if (c.indexOf(name) == 0) return c.substring(name.length,c.length);
    }
    return "";
}
</script>
```

Add this function to your web pages if it has not already been added.

12.3 Implementing the Tracking Code

The next step is to implement the code to perform the tracking. The blocking code outlined in the previous chapter was implemented as follows:

```
var detector = function() {
    setTimeout(function() {

        if(!document.getElementsByClassName) return;
```

Tracking the Visitor Response Rate

```
        var ads =
                document.getElementsByClassName('banner_ad'),
            ad  = ads[ads.length - 1];

        if(!ad || ad.innerHTML.length == 0
                    || ad.clientHeight === 0) {
                $("#myModal").modal("show");
                $("#myModal").on('hide.bs.modal', function () {
                        window.location.reload();
                });
            }
        }, 2000);
}
```

As currently implemented, the page is configured to display the modal dialog each time the page loads and an ad blocker is detected. Begin my modifying this code as follows:

```
var detector = function() {
    setTimeout(function() {

        if(!document.getElementsByClassName) return;
        var ads =
                document.getElementsByClassName('banner_ad'),
            ad  = ads[ads.length - 1];

        if(!ad || ad.innerHTML.length == 0
                    || ad.clientHeight === 0) {
            $("#myModal").modal("show");
            $("#myModal").on('hide.bs.modal', function () {
                    window.location.reload();
            });

            if (getCookie("requestmade") == "") {
                var date = new Date();
                date.setTime(date.getTime() + (30*1000));
                var expires = "expires="+date.toUTCString();
                document.cookie = "requestmade=true; " + expires;

                ga('send', {
                    'hitType': 'event',
                    'eventCategory': 'RemovalRequests',
                    'eventAction': 'Requested',
                    'nonInteraction': 1
```

87

Tracking the Visitor Response Rate

```
                });
            }
        }, 2000);
    }
```

If no "requestmade" cookie is detected, the cookie is written to the visitor's browser and an event sent to Google Analytics using a category name of "RemovalRequests" and an event named "Requested".

Code now needs to be added to handle the situation where the cookie is present but the ad blocker is disabled:

```
var detector = function() {
    setTimeout(function() {

        if(!document.getElementsByClassName) return;
        var ads =
                document.getElementsByClassName('banner_ad'),
            ad = ads[ads.length - 1];

        if(!ad || ad.innerHTML.length == 0
                    || ad.clientHeight === 0) {
            $("#myModal").modal("show");
            $("#myModal").on('hide.bs.modal', function () {
                    window.location.reload();
            });

            if (getCookie("requestmade") == "") {
                var date = new Date();
                date.setTime(date.getTime() + (30*1000));
                var expires = "expires="+date.toUTCString();
                document.cookie = "requestmade=true; " + expires;

                ga('send', {
                    'hitType': 'event',
                    'eventCategory': 'RemovalRequests',
                    'eventAction': 'Requested',
                    'nonInteraction': 1
                });
        } else {
                if (getCookie("requestmade") != "") {
                    ga('send', {
```

88

Tracking the Visitor Response Rate

```
                    'hitType': 'event',
                    'eventCategory': 'RemovalRequests',
                    'eventAction': 'Complied',
                    'nonInteraction': 1
                });
            }
        }
    }, 2000);
}
```

The above changes represent the code that gets called when no ad blocker is detected. If the "requestmade" cookie exists then the visitor has seen the dialog and turned off ad blocking. This fact is recorded via an analytics event, once again assigned to the "RemovalRequests" category, but this time using an event named "Complied".

12.4 Reviewing the Results

Although Google Analytics will begin recording and reporting data almost immediately, the amount of time it will take to gather meaningful statistics will vary depending on the volume of traffic to the website. View the statistics by opening Google Analytics in a browser window and displaying the reporting information for your website. Within the left hand navigation panel, select *Behavior -> Events -> Top Event* to display information about the RemovalRequests event category.

Click on the RemovalRequests category to view the data for the individual event actions. To access a graphical view of the event actions data, click on one of the buttons located in the right hand side of the toolbar:

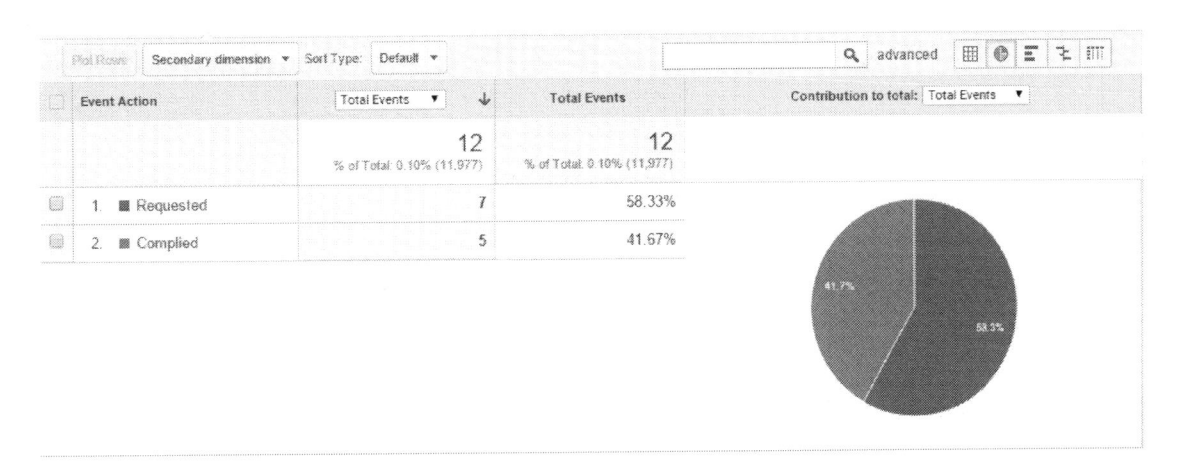

Figure 12-1

89

12.5 Summary

It is important to carefully track the effectiveness of any campaign designed to encourage site visitors to disable ad blocking, particularly when denying access to those unwilling to whitelist your site. If the majority of visitors simply leave your site rather than turn off ad blocking there are certainly other more profitable approaches to dealing with ad blocking. It is, after all, much easier to find ways to earn revenue from a visitor that you have than a visitor you have lost.

This chapter has covered the steps involved in using Google Analytics to track and quantify the success rate of an ad blocker removal request campaign.

Chapter 13

13. Truncating Web Page Content

A variation on the theme of denying access in the presence of an ad blocker involves displaying an abridged version of the content together with a message instructing the visitor to disable ad blocking in order to access the full page.

In this chapter the steps to truncate the content of a web page when an active ad blocker is enabled will be covered.

13.1 Truncated Content

Rather than deny access through the presentation of a modal dialog, the concept of truncated content involves displaying just enough of the content for the visitor to fully appreciate the value of the website and to become sufficiently engaged to willingly disable ad blocking to access the remainder of the page.

Figure 13-1 shows an example rendering of this strategy in action:

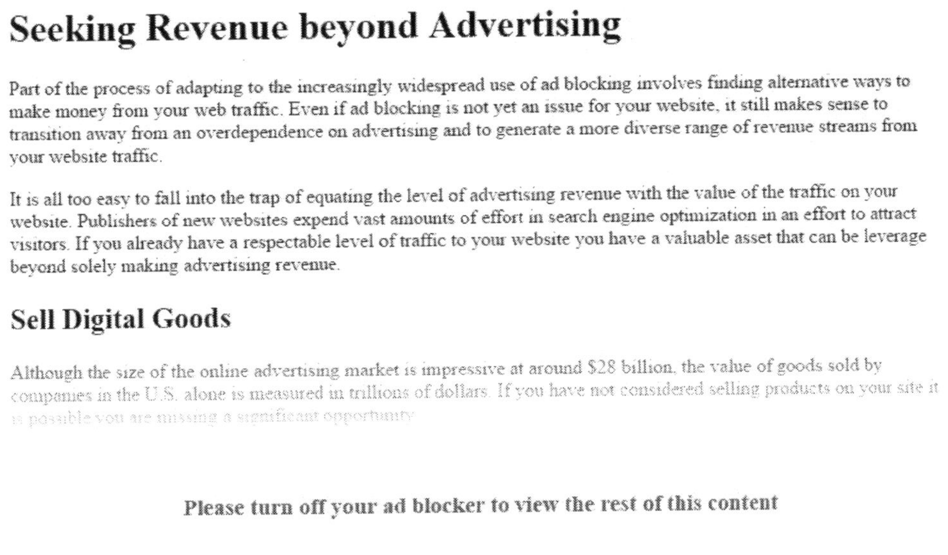

Seeking Revenue beyond Advertising

Part of the process of adapting to the increasingly widespread use of ad blocking involves finding alternative ways to make money from your web traffic. Even if ad blocking is not yet an issue for your website, it still makes sense to transition away from an overdependence on advertising and to generate a more diverse range of revenue streams from your website traffic.

It is all too easy to fall into the trap of equating the level of advertising revenue with the value of the traffic on your website. Publishers of new websites expend vast amounts of effort in search engine optimization in an effort to attract visitors. If you already have a respectable level of traffic to your website you have a valuable asset that can be leverage beyond solely making advertising revenue.

Sell Digital Goods

Although the size of the online advertising market is impressive at around $28 billion, the value of goods sold by companies in the U.S. alone is measured in trillions of dollars. If you have not considered selling products on your site it is possible you are missing a significant opportunity.

Please turn off your ad blocker to view the rest of this content

Figure 13-1

Truncating Web Page Content

In the above example, only the first few paragraphs of the page are displayed entirely, with the content gradually fading out in the third paragraph. The visitor is then encouraged to disable ad blocking in order to view the remainder of the page.

The amount of content to display while ad blocking remains active will vary depending on the content of the site. To avoid the visitor feeling misled, however, it is recommended that the cutoff point appear above or immediately below the fold (the "area above the fold" being the part of the web page that is visible without the necessity to scroll). Allowing the visitor to read 90% of the page before finding out that access is denied to the remaining 10% may, after all, leave the visitor with an unnecessarily adverse opinion of your website.

13.2 Truncating the Content

This chapter makes the assumption that the main content of the web page is contained within a <div> element with an id of "container", for example:

```
<div id="container">
         Main Content Here
</div>
```

It is also assumed that the container has been configured with relative positioning:

```
<style>
#container {
    position:relative;
    padding:0px;
    margin:0px;
}
</style>
```

The first step in this example is to implement some JavaScript code so that the content of a web page is truncated to a specified number of characters on the detection of an ad blocker. For this purpose, the standard ad blocker detection code will first be used as originally introduced in the chapter entitled *Basic Ad Blocker Detection*:

```
<div class="banner_ad"> </div>
<script src=
"https://ajax.googleapis.com/ajax/libs/jquery/1.12.0/jquery.min.js">
</script>
<script>
(function() {
```

Truncating Web Page Content

```
        var detector = function() {
            setTimeout(function() {

                if(!document.getElementsByClassName) return;
                var ads =
                        document.getElementsByClassName('banner_ad'),
                    ad = ads[ads.length - 1];

                if(!ad || ad.innerHTML.length == 0
                            || ad.clientHeight === 0) {


                }

            }, 2000);
        }

        /* Add a page load listener */
        if(window.addEventListener) {
            window.addEventListener('load', detector, false);
        }
})();
</script>
```

The code to truncate the content needs to be added to the body of the *if* statement so that it is executed on the detection of an ad blocker:

```
·
·
·
if(!ad || ad.innerHTML.length == 0
                    || ad.clientHeight === 0) {

                if(!ad || ad.innerHTML.length == 0
                            || ad.clientHeight === 0) {
    $('.container').each(function() {
      var length = 1600;
      var details = $(this);
      var original_html = details.html();
      var truncated_html = $.trim(original_html).substring(0,
          length).split(" ").slice(0, -1).join(" ") + " ";
      details.html(truncated_html);
    });
```

93

Truncating Web Page Content

```
    }
    .
    .
    .
```

The above code works through every element in the page with an id of "container". For each matching element the HTML content is extracted, truncated to a length of 1600 characters and then placed back into the element so that it appears in abbreviated form within the browser window.

13.3 Adding the Ad Blocker Whitelist Request

Now that the content is being truncated for ad blocking visitors, the next step is to insert a message immediately after the truncated content element informing the visitor that ad blocking must be turned off in order to continue reading the content. For the purposes of this example, the message is centered, displayed in green using a larger font which, in turn, requires an additional CSS style entry:

```
<style>
#container {
    position:relative;
    padding:0px;
    margin:0px;
}

.ab_message {
    font-size: x-large;
    text-align: center;
    color: green;
}
</style>
```

Next, extend the truncation code to insert the message after the container element as follows:

```
    .
    .
    .
$('.container').each(function(){
    var length = 1600;
    var details = $(this);
    var original_html = details.html();
```

```
    var truncated_html = $.trim(original_html).substring(0,
length).split(" ").slice(0, -1).join(" ") + " ";
    details.html(truncated_html);
    $('<p class="ab_message">Please whitelist this site in your ad
blocker and reload to continue</p>').insertAfter('.container');
  });
```

At this point in the example, a page containing more than 1600 characters of content will resemble that shown in Figure 13-2 below when loaded into a browser with an ad blocker installed and enabled:

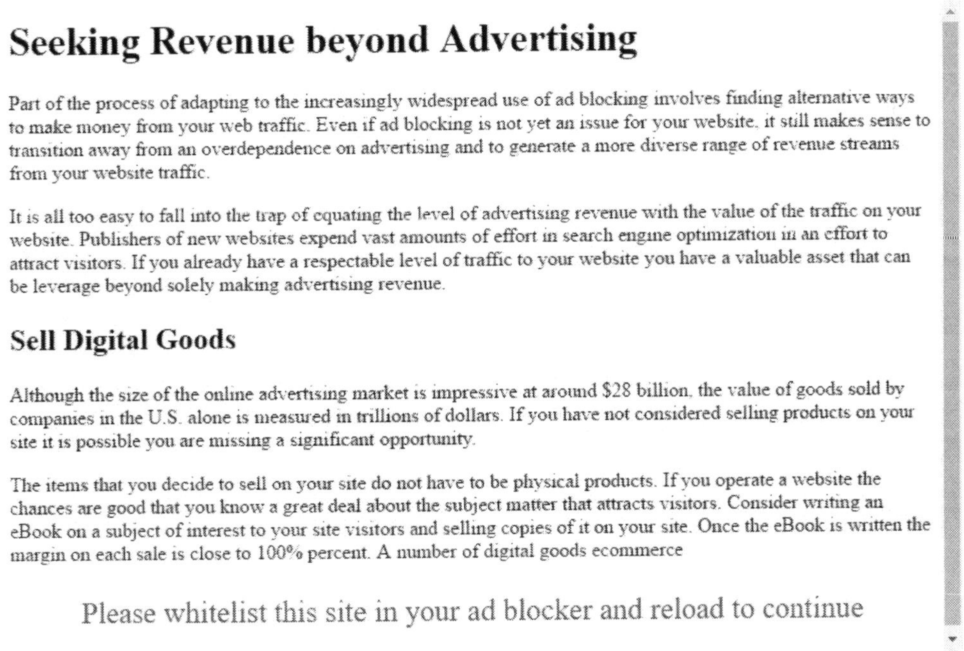

Seeking Revenue beyond Advertising

Part of the process of adapting to the increasingly widespread use of ad blocking involves finding alternative ways to make money from your web traffic. Even if ad blocking is not yet an issue for your website, it still makes sense to transition away from an overdependence on advertising and to generate a more diverse range of revenue streams from your website traffic.

It is all too easy to fall into the trap of equating the level of advertising revenue with the value of the traffic on your website. Publishers of new websites expend vast amounts of effort in search engine optimization in an effort to attract visitors. If you already have a respectable level of traffic to your website you have a valuable asset that can be leverage beyond solely making advertising revenue.

Sell Digital Goods

Although the size of the online advertising market is impressive at around $28 billion, the value of goods sold by companies in the U.S. alone is measured in trillions of dollars. If you have not considered selling products on your site it is possible you are missing a significant opportunity.

The items that you decide to sell on your site do not have to be physical products. If you operate a website the chances are good that you know a great deal about the subject matter that attracts visitors. Consider writing an eBook on a subject of interest to your site visitors and selling copies of it on your site. Once the eBook is written the margin on each sale is close to 100% percent. A number of digital goods ecommerce

Please whitelist this site in your ad blocker and reload to continue

Figure 13-2

Whitelisting the site or disabling the ad blocker and then reloading the page will cause the entire page content to appear.

13.4 Implementing the Fading Effect

The fading effect presents a less abrupt termination to the content and provides an intuitive visual indication that more content is available. The final step in this chapter is to implement this effect by overlaying a linear gradient on top of the container element.

Truncating Web Page Content

Begin by declaring the style for the linear gradient (a different entry is needed for each of the major web browsers). This declaration can be added within the previously implemented <style> section as follows:

```
<style>
#container {
    position:relative;
    padding:0px;
    margin:0px;
}

.ab_message {
    font-size: x-large;
    text-align: center;
    color: green;
}

#gradient {
    position:absolute;
    z-index:2;
    right:0; bottom:20; left:0;
    height:30%;

    background: -moz-linear-gradient(top,  rgba(255,255,255,0) 0%, rgba(255,255,255,1) 70%);
    background: -webkit-gradient(linear, left top, left bottom, color-stop(0%,rgba(255,255,255,0)), color-stop(70%,rgba(255,255,255,1)));
    background: -webkit-linear-gradient(top,  rgba(255,255,255,0) 0%,rgba(255,255,255,1) 70%);
    background: -o-linear-gradient(top,  rgba(255,255,255,0) 0%,rgba(255,255,255,1) 70%);
    background: -ms-linear-gradient(top,  rgba(255,255,255,0) 0%,rgba(255,255,255,1) 70%);
    background: linear-gradient(to bottom,  rgba(255,255,255,0) 0%,rgba(255,255,255,1) 70%);
    filter: progid:DXImageTransform.Microsoft.gradient( startColorstr='#00ffffff', endColorstr='#ffffff',GradientType=0 );
}
</style>
```

Next, a <div> element using the *gradient* id now needs to be appended to the end of the truncated content as follows:

Truncating Web Page Content

```
.
.
.
$('.container').each(function(){
    var length = 1600;
    var details = $(this);
    var original_html = details.html();
    var truncated_html = $.trim(original_html).substring(0,
        length).split(" ").slice(0, -1).join(" ") + " ";
    details.html(truncated_html);
    details.append('<div id="gradient"></div>');
    $( '<p class="ab_message">Please whitelist this site in your ad blocker and reload to continue</p>' ).insertAfter('.container');
});
.
.
.
```

With the truncation code now fully implemented the truncated content will fade out before the request message appears:

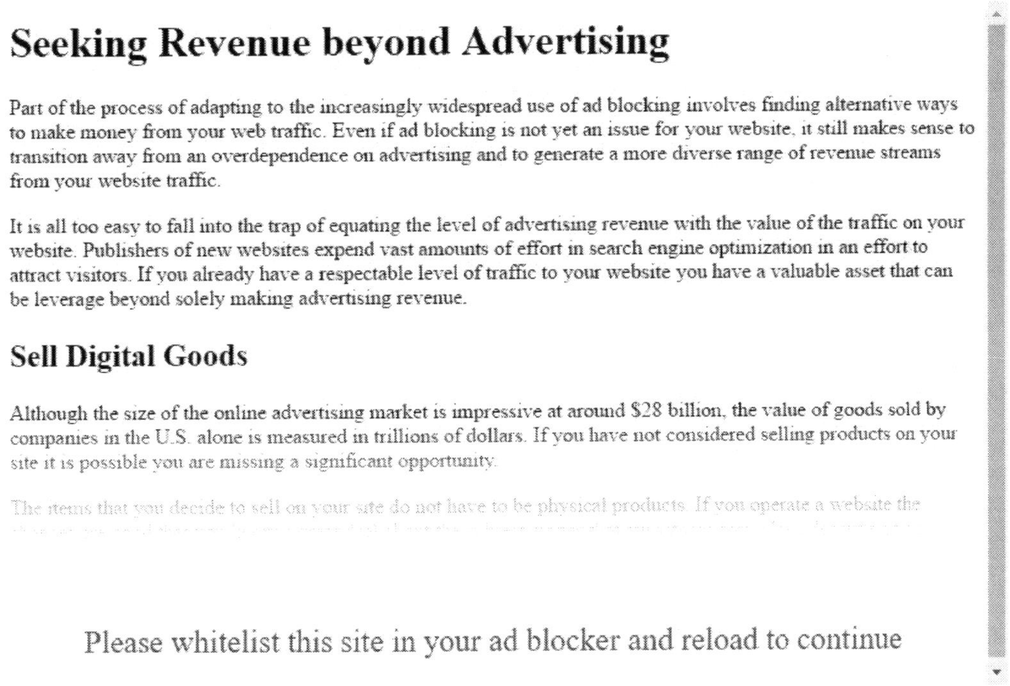

Figure 13-3

97

See it in Action

http://www.techotopia.com/survival/truncate.html

13.5 Summary

An alternative to denying access to the content of a web page in the presence of an ad blocker is to display part of the content followed by a request to turn off ad blocking in order to gain access to the remainder of the page. This approach has the advantage of conveying the value of the content to the site visitor before imposing any access restriction. This technique can be achieved by truncating the content within specific elements of the page and placing a message immediately after the point of truncation. A gradient effect may also be added to make the termination of content less abrupt and to visually suggest the availability of more content.

14. Participating in the Acceptable Ads Initiative

The Acceptable Ads initiative is a program initiated by Eyeo GmbH, the company behind the AdBlock Plus ad blocker. The initiative provides a mechanism by which web publishers are able to apply to Eyeo to have ad elements that meet specified criteria whitelisted so that they appear even when a site visitor has AdBlock Plus installed and enabled.

This chapter will introduce the Acceptable Ads initiative (including the controversy surrounding it) and outline the requirements and steps that can be taken to participate in this program. The next chapter, entitled *Running Acceptable Ads with PageFair*, will introduce an alternative approach to using acceptable ads.

14.1 The Acceptable Ads Initiative

The Acceptable Ads initiative was started in 2011 ostensibly to provide a way for web publishers to generate advertising revenue by running ads that comply with specific criteria in terms of content and positioning. Such ad elements, once approved by Eyeo, are added to the Acceptable Ads list.

When a user installs AdBlock Plus, an option in the filter lists settings page labelled *Allow some non-intrusive advertising* (highlighted in Figure 14-1) is enabled by default:

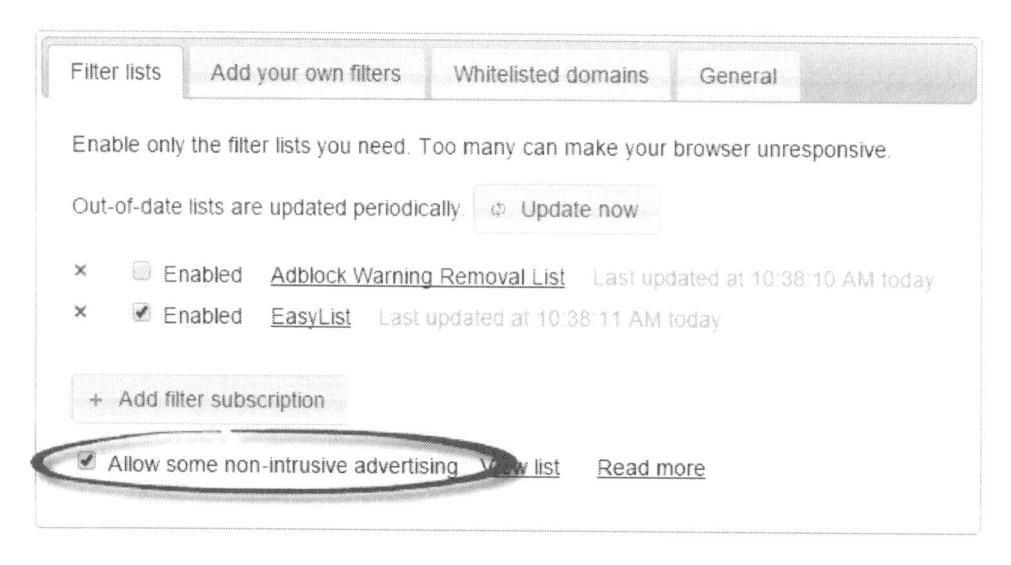

Figure 14-1

Unless the user disables this option, AdBlock Plus will not block those ads on your website that have been approved as meeting the Acceptable Ads criteria.

14.2 The Acceptable Ads Controversy – A Publisher's Friend or Foe?

Before discussing whether web publishers should make efforts to comply with the Acceptable Ads initiative, it is worthwhile taking time to cover some of the controversy surrounding the initiative.

If you are a small to medium-sized web publisher then it costs nothing to participate in the program. Large publishers, however, are required to pay to run Acceptable Ads. If participating in the program will result in your site receiving more than 10 million additional ad impressions per month your site is considered a large entity and must pay 30% of any additional revenue generated as a result of using Acceptable Ads (Google reportedly paid $25 million to participate). This makes the initiative unpopular with several groups. The advertising industry claims that this is a form of extortion targeting large publishers and only serves to fund the creation of more advanced ad blocking technology. Large publishers, of course, resent having to pay for the privilege of displaying ads on their own sites. Finally, the developers of competing ad blocking solutions consider the displaying of Acceptable Ads to be betrayal of the goal of eliminating all advertising from every website on the internet.

14.3 Are Acceptable Ads an Acceptable Option?

For small and medium-sized web publishers the decision as to whether or not to participate in the Acceptable Ads program is easier. The advantages are that the program is free to join and, once accepted, your web site will begin to generate revenue from ads that would previously have been blocked. Since no payment is required to participate at this level the ethical dilemma of funding ad blocking technology is not of concern.

It is important to be aware that this strategy, though worthwhile considering, does not resolve all of the problems associated with ad blocking. Even if implemented, some issues will remain outstanding:

- Only AdBlock Plus makes use of the Acceptable Ads list. All other ad blocking solutions will continue to block the ads.
- Users of AdBlock Plus have the option to turn off the Acceptable Ads option, causing the ads to be blocked.
- The initiative is essentially designed to display ads, albeit less intrusive ones, to visitors who dislike ads so much they have installed an ad blocker. While less of a problem for CPM based ads, it is likely that the click-through rates for CPC based ads will be lower for these ads.

Shortcomings aside, it is important to keep in mind that AdBlock Plus is among the most popular ad blocking solutions on the market today. This combined with the fact that Acceptable Ads are enabled by default within AdBlock Plus means that many users will leave the option enabled out of inertia.

Unless you can find a more profitable way to make use of otherwise blocked ad space, the Acceptable Ads program, despite some negative publicity, is probably worth trying. You can, after all, stop participating at any time.

14.4 Acceptable Ads

The criteria used to decide whether an ad is eligible for inclusion as an Acceptable Ad can be divided into three groups, each of which is summarized below. Since these criteria may be subject to change, it is worth checking on the latest requirements at:

https://adblockplus.org/en/acceptable-ads#criteria

14.4.1 Placement Criteria

An Acceptable Ad must be positioned at the top, side or bottom of the main content of the web page, should clearly be an advertisement and must be labelled with text that makes clear it is an ad (for example the word "advertisement" placed above the ad would adequately meet this requirement).

14.4.2 Size Criteria

An ad placed above the content must not exceed 200px in height. Ads positioned to the side of the main content are restricted to a maximum width of 350px. Ads placed below the main content cannot exceed 400px in height.

Ads appearing above the fold must not occupy more than 15% of the visible area of the web page. When appearing below the fold, the ad must not exceed 25% of the visible area.

14.4.3 Content Criteria

The content of the ad should ideally be text-based (Google AdSense ads configured as text only, for example, will generally meet this requirement). In addition, text ads must not make excessive use of distracting colors.

Image ads must be static and unobtrusive (no animation is permitted) and will be considered for inclusion on a case-by-case basis.

14.4.4 Ads Not Considered to be Eligible

The following lists verbatim the types of ads that are not considered to be eligible for the inclusion in the program:

- Ads that visibly load new ads if the Primary Content does not change
- Ads with excessive or non user-initiated hover effects
- Animated ads
- Autoplay-sound or video ads
- Expanding ads
- Generally oversized image ads
- Interstitial page ads
- Overlay ads
- Overlay in-video ads
- Pop-ups
- Pop-unders
- Pre-roll video ads
- Rich media ads (e.g. Flash ads, Shockwave ads, etc.)

14.5 Getting your Ads Approved

Once you believe you have compliant ads running on your site, begin by completing and submitting the following application form:

https://eyeo.com/acceptable-ads-application.html

Enter the URL for a page on your site where the acceptable ads are active. Two additional URLs may be entered if you have pages with different layouts that also contain acceptable ads. Enter any comments that you feel are necessary (such as explaining the locations where the ads appear and the ad networks through which the ads are being served).

Once the application form has been submitted, Eyeo will contact you at some point in the future to verify the ads for which you are seeking approval and outline changes that may be required before approval is granted. When the ads meet the criteria you will be required to enter into an agreement with Eyeo, after which the whitelisting of your ads will be posted the AdBlock Plus Acceptable Ads proposal forum at:

https://adblockplus.org/forum/viewforum.php?f=12

At the same time that the proposal is posted to the forum your ads will be whitelisted within the Acceptable Ads list. According to Eyeo, it can take up to 10 days from the point that your ads are deemed to be acceptable before the whitelisting is implemented.

14.6 Keeping Track of the Results

Assuming you reach the point where your website is participating in the Acceptable Ads initiative, it will be important to keep track of the effectiveness of this strategy. Consider using ad blocker detection and ad reinsertion to run different ad units depending on whether an ad blocker is enabled. This will allow you to monitor the amount of revenue that is coming directly from ads that would otherwise have been blocked.

Also consider adjusting the detection code to track the percentage of visitors with ad blocking enabled for which the ad is hidden. This will provide an indication of the number of visitors who have turned off Acceptable Ads in AdBlock Plus, or are using an ad blocker that does not support the Acceptable Ads initiative.

Low revenue and a high percentage of blocking may be an indication that better use can be made of the ad space.

14.7 Summary

The acceptable ads initiative is a program introduced by the company responsible for the AdBlock Plus ad blocker. The program defines criteria for the content, size and positioning of ads on a web page that are deemed to be acceptable for display even when the AdBlock Plus ad blocker is enabled. Once the ads on a website have been submitted and approved by the program, those ads will appear to visitors using AdBlock Plus. The displaying of acceptable ads, however, is only supported by AdBlock Plus, and may be turned off by users that do not wish to see any advertising.

Although subject to some controversy from the advertising industry and large web publishers, there is little downside for small and medium sized publishers (aside from the time and effort involved in seeking ad approval) to trying out the acceptable ads program.

15. Running Acceptable Ads with PageFair

PageFair is a company that is advocating a non-confrontational approach to dealing with ad blocking by making use of the acceptable ads initiative. As outlined in the previous chapter, it is possible to participate directly in the acceptable ads program, though it takes some time and effort. PageFair provides a way to instantly begin running acceptable ads on your website without needing to go through the approval process with Eyeo.

This chapter will introduce the service provided by PageFair and outline some advantages and disadvantages of using this service.

15.1 What is PageFair?

PageFair was introduced briefly in the *Assessing the Damage* chapter of this book. The company essentially provides two services, the first being the ability to measure the percentage of visitors to your website using ad blocking.

The second service offered by PageFair provides a way to display ads that meet the acceptable ads standard on your site without the need to go through the approval process.

15.2 How to Run PageFair Ads

Once you have created a PageFair account and set up a website entry, the code listed under *Basic Setup* in the setup page of the dashboard will need to be placed on each page of your website (this step is not necessary if you already added this code in the *Assessing the Damage* chapter of this book):

Running Acceptable Ads with PageFair

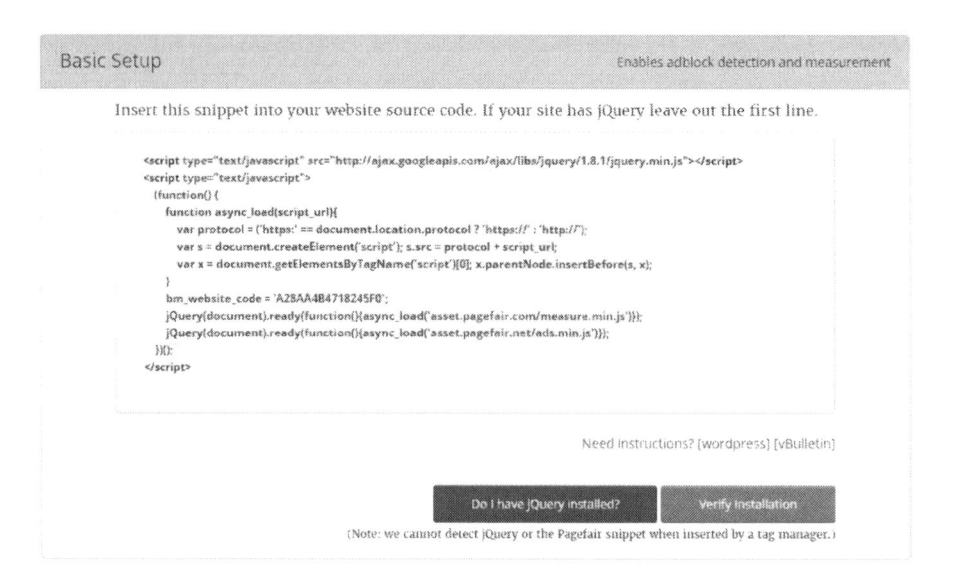

Figure 15-1

Once the code has been added to the pages of your website, use the *Verify Installation* button to make sure that the code is functioning.

The *Full Setup* section of the setup dashboard page allows ad spaces to be generated based on ad size. Figure 15-2, for example, shows two skyscraper ad spaces already configured within the PageFair dashboard:

Figure 15-2

To create a new ad space, select the ad size (marked as A in the above figure) from the menu before clicking on the Add button. Once you have added an ad space, copy the ad space tag code displayed in the ad space list (B) and paste it into your web page so that it is located next to the code for an existing ad of the same size on your web site.

Within the PageFair dashboard, select the Ads tab and use the *Targeting category* menu to select the advertising category that most closely matches your website content (for example automotive, technology or games).

With the target category set and the ad space tags embedded in your web pages, the PageFair system will begin functioning.

15.3 PageFair Network Ads

Once configured, the PageFair detection code will detect the presence of an ad blocker and display an ad from the PageFair Ad Network in place of the blocked ad. Ads from the PageFair network are text only ads that resemble that shown in Figure 15-3 below:

Figure 15-3

Running Acceptable Ads with PageFair

To generate revenue reports for PageFair ads running on your site, select the Reports tab and choose the *Ad Performance* menu option. Select a date range before clicking on the View report button:

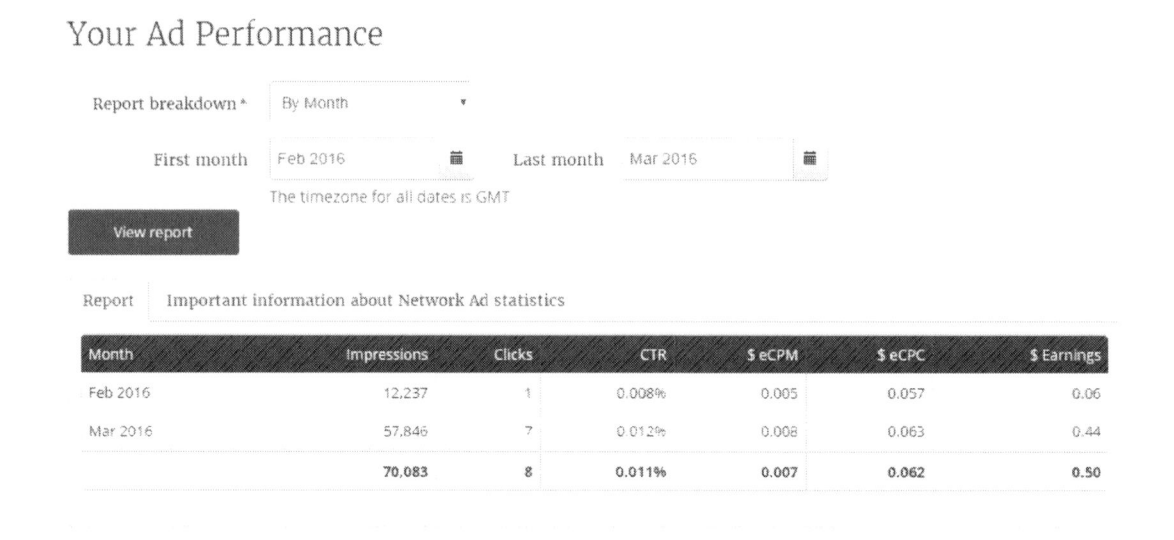

Your Ad Performance

Month	Impressions	Clicks	CTR	$ eCPM	$ eCPC	$ Earnings
Feb 2016	12,237	1	0.008%	0.005	0.057	0.06
Mar 2016	57,846	7	0.012%	0.008	0.063	0.44
	70,083	8	0.011%	0.007	0.062	0.50

Figure 15-4

As can be seen from the report, all PageFair network ads are Cost-Per-Click (CPC) based ads.

15.4 Running Your Own Ads

In addition to running ads from PageFair, it is also possible to create and run your own ads from within the PageFair dashboard. These ads are text based and will be similar in format to the ads from the PageFair network as illustrated in Figure 15-3 above.

To design your own ads, select the Ads tab within the PageFair dashboard, scroll down to *Create Your Own Ads* and click on the *Create A New Ad* button. Fill in the information for the new ad using the ad creation tool as illustrated in Figure 15-5.

If the ad you are running has either a CPC or CPM value, enter this into the form. PageFair will use this information to ensure that your ad will appear whenever the value is greater than an equivalent ad within the PageFair network. Your ad will also run when no PageFair network ad is available for your site.

Figure 15-5

This feature of PageFair can be used to display ads from direct advertising partners, used to promote your own products and services, or even to display a message asking visitors to turn off ad blocking.

15.5 PageFair Pros and Cons

The key advantage of PageFair is that it allows you to quickly and easily run ads that conform to the acceptable ads standard by placing simple tags into the pages of your website. This avoids the need to implement ad detection code, source acceptable ads to display and work through the acceptable ads approval process. Assuming that adding these tags to your site does not require significant effort, PageFair allows ads to begin running within minutes.

While PageFair has clear benefits, it is far from a complete solution to the problems caused by ad blockers. As previously discussed, acceptable ads are only supported by AdBlock Plus, and even those users have the ability to disable the feature. This means that only a subset of visitors using ad blocking will see the alternate ads served by PageFair. Similarly, any ads of your own that you create and serve within PageFair will be blocked by most other ad blocking tools.

Another issue is that the PageFair ad network is unlikely to be able to fill all of your blocked ad inventory and those ads that do run appear to have very low CPC rates. It is quite possible that the PageFair ad network is still evolving and that higher CPC rates will be available in the future, but you may find that using ad reinsertion to run your own ads, or working directly with Eyeo to display Google AdSense text ads as acceptable ads may prove more profitable.

Given the ease and speed with which PageFair can be set up it is certainly worth trying, if only as a stopgap while exploring more advanced options.

15.6 Summary

PageFair provides a quick and easy way to run acceptable ads on your website. Ads may either be sourced from PageFair, or created directly from within the PageFair dashboard. PageFair offers the advantage of an easy way to participate in the acceptable ads initiative, though it is important to be aware that CPC revenue and click-through rates for PageFair sourced ads are very low and that the ads will only be visible to users of AdBlock Plus who have not disabled the option to whitelist acceptable ads.

Chapter 16

16. Running Native Advertising

Although relatively new, native advertising is an area that is gaining interest within the web publishing industry. In particular it is increasing in popularity because it tends to result in a greater level of responsiveness from website visitors than traditional online advertising and, if implemented correctly, can be immune to ad blocking. These strengths make native advertising a worthwhile option to consider as part of a strategy to address ad blocking.

16.1 What is Native Advertising?

Native advertising, as will be covered later in the chapter, can take a variety of different forms. The official definition of native advertising, as stated in Wikipedia, reads as follows:

"Native advertising is a type of advertising, usually online but feasibly elsewhere, that matches the form and function of the platform upon which it appears."

It helps to break this definition down into its constituent parts when explaining what it means. By *advertising* we are, of course, referring to paid content, the purpose of which is to promote an organization, product or service. The term *platform* refers to the medium through which the advertisement is presented to the potential customer. For the purposes of this book this is assumed to be a website, but applies equally to apps and print publications. When the definition declares that native ads match the *form and function* of the platform, this means that the advertisement not only matches the visual design of the website, but also looks, feels and behaves like the site's own content.

As opposed to the traditional ad units that appear in the form of a banner at the top of the page or a skyscraper in a side bar, native advertising is typically integrated into the main content of the website. A native ad can range from sponsored links in search results through to an entire web page article or news item designed to engage the reader with relevant content while also promoting the interests of the advertiser.

Native ads are believed to be more effective at gaining visitor attention and engagement. Because native ads make up part of the main content of a web page, they are often harder to remove using ad blocking technology.

111

Running Native Advertising

Despite the need to blend seamlessly with the content of the page, native content should not be deceptive. Native advertisements should always be disclosed using wording such as "Sponsored", "Promoted", "Sponsored Content", "Suggested Links", "You might also like" etc.

16.2 Types of Native Ad Content

The Interactive Advertising Bureau (IAB) produced the Native Advertising Playbook in 2013 to outline a number of different categories of native ad.

16.2.1 In-Feed Ads

An in-feed ad is typically presented in story form and appears within the main body of the web page. It is designed to match the surrounding content and can link either to another page within the website, or to an external page. The example shown in Figure 16-1, represents a typical in-feed native ad for gardening equipment embedded within the list of news items on the Yahoo News web page:

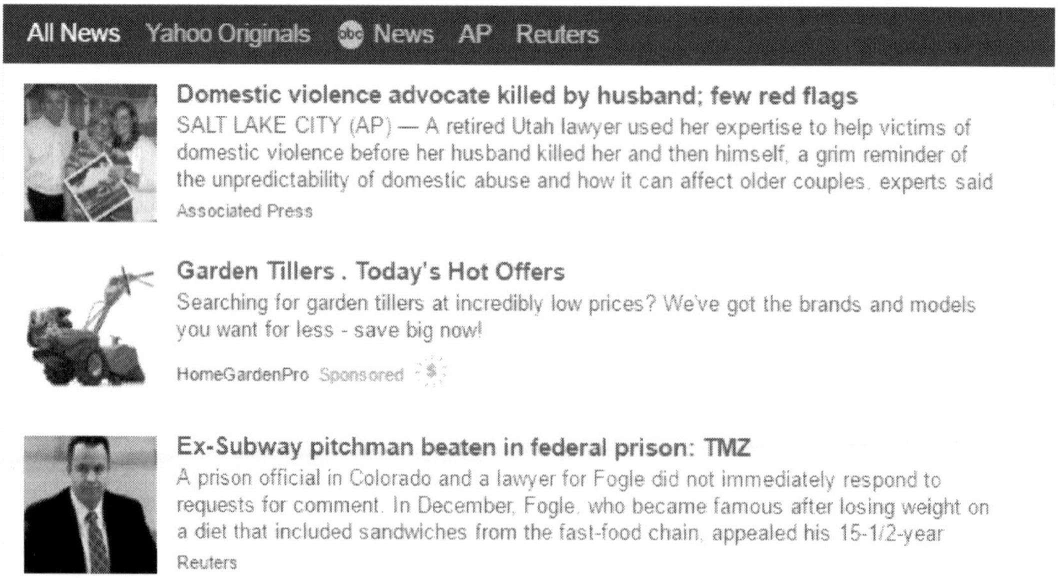

Figure 16-1

Such content is usually disclosed as being advertising by the inclusion of text that reads "Promoted", "Sponsored" or "Sponsored Content".

16.2.2 Search Ads

The sponsored entries that appear at the top of a Google search results page are a prime example of native search ads. Aside from the declaration that these are ads, the form and function of the entries match that of the organic search results. Figure 16-2, for example, shows a combination of native search ads and an organic search result:

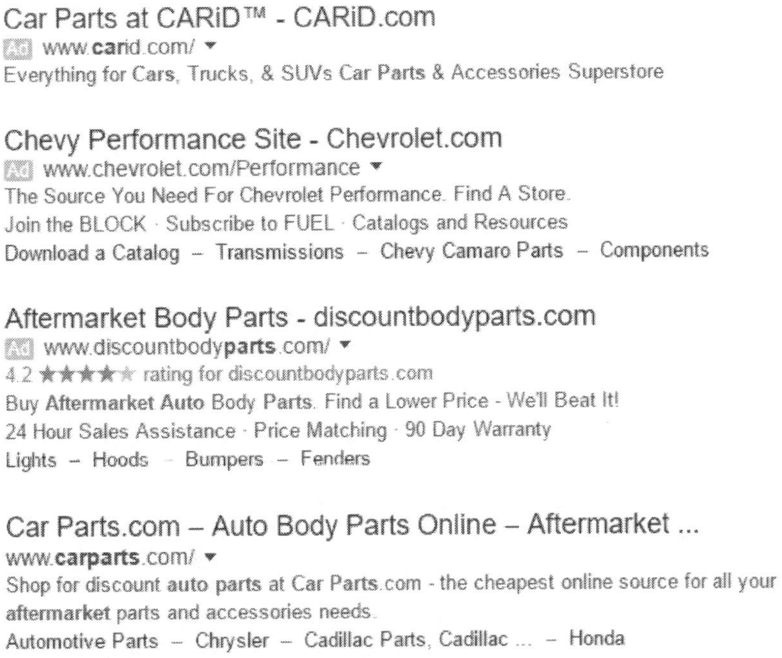

Car Parts at CARiD™ - CARiD.com
[Ad] www.carid.com/ ▼
Everything for Cars, Trucks, & SUVs Car Parts & Accessories Superstore

Chevy Performance Site - Chevrolet.com
[Ad] www.chevrolet.com/Performance ▼
The Source You Need For Chevrolet Performance. Find A Store.
Join the BLOCK · Subscribe to FUEL · Catalogs and Resources
Download a Catalog — Transmissions — Chevy Camaro Parts — Components

Aftermarket Body Parts - discountbodyparts.com
[Ad] www.discountbodyparts.com/ ▼
4.2 ★★★★☆ rating for discountbodyparts.com
Buy Aftermarket Auto Body Parts. Find a Lower Price - We'll Beat It!
24 Hour Sales Assistance · Price Matching · 90 Day Warranty
Lights — Hoods — Bumpers — Fenders

Car Parts.com – Auto Body Parts Online – Aftermarket ...
www.carparts.com/ ▼
Shop for discount auto parts at Car Parts.com - the cheapest online source for all your aftermarket parts and accessories needs.
Automotive Parts — Chrysler — Cadillac Parts, Cadillac ... — Honda

Figure 16-2

16.2.3 Recommendation Widgets

Recommendation widgets typically provide a list of recommended content found on other websites pages with a declaration which often reads "You might also like", "Recommended for you" or "From around the web". Figure 16-3 shows two items listed within a recommendation widget. This type of native advertising can be used by advertisers to drive traffic to a web site or to promote a product or service:

AROUND THE WEB

Comparing 4 High-Paying Rewards Cards. And The Winner Is...
LendingTree

Mind Blown! 15 Sports Wardrobe Malfunctions -- #10 Is Hard To Believe
The Brofessional

Sponsored Links by Taboola

Figure 16-3

16.2.4 Promoted Listings

Generally used on websites designed to sell products and services (as opposed to being primarily content based), promoted listings are advertisements for products or services that link to a third party page where the visitor can make a purchase. In this scenario, the web publisher might write a review of a product and include a promoted listing for the product. This listing will include a link or button allowing the user to click through and buy the product, with the publisher typically earning a commission on the sale:

The Best Open-Back Headphones under $500

📅 NOVEMBER 19, 2015   👤 BRENT BUTTERWORTH

Tweet   Pocket 75   G+1 26   Pin it   Email

If a serious music lover asked me what open-back audiophile headphones to buy and wanted to spend less than $500, I'd recommend the HiFiMan HE400S. These aren't cheap, yet emerged as the favorite when our panel of audio professionals spent 60 hours evaluating 29 open-back and semi-open-back headphones—nearly every model available for less than $500. Among those, the HE400S headphones were the only ones that we all agreed deserved a high ranking.

Our pick
HiFiMan HE400S
Unbelievably spacious and natural sound—along with unusual versatility—makes these the only open-back headphone all of our panelists loved.

$300 from Amazon
$300 from B&H

16.2.5 In-Ad

An in-ad native advertisement is designed to fit within a traditional ad sized container (such as a banner or skyscraper) and, like a traditional ad, is placed outside of the natural content of the page. The content of the ad must be contextually relevant to the rest of the content of the page.

16.3 Implementing Native Advertising

There are a number of approaches that can be taken when implementing native advertising on your website. If you already have a direct relationship with companies that run traditional advertising on your site, approach those partners and suggest that they produce in-feed native ad content suitable for placement on your site. If you do not yet sell your ad space inventory direct to advertisers, give serious thought to doing so. Begin by creating a media kit and running ads on your own site seeking potential direct advertisers. Also consider using social media and running ads on Google using appropriate keywords to attract the attention of advertisers.

Also, consider generating your own content that can be used to provide context for a promoted product listing. Write impartial product reviews, for example, and include options to purchase those items using programs such as Amazon Associates or Best Buy Affiliates.

Alternatively, the option is available to partner with one of the many native advertising companies such as Taboola, Outbrain and ShareThrough, though keep in mind that some of the native advertising provided by these companies will be targeted by ad blockers in the same way as traditional ads. That being said, both Taboola and Outbrain have paid to join the acceptable ads program so you may have success getting some of those ads whitelisted on your site for visitors using AdBlock Plus. Be sure to carefully vet any potential native ad providers before investing time and effort into this approach. In particular, seek assurances that native ad content provided will be relevant to your website. Some native ad providers, particularly those providing recommendation widgets, have a tendency to display low quality so called "click-bait" recommendations that may not be the best fit for your website.

16.4 Summary

Native advertising is generally identified as achieving greater levels of response and engagement that traditional forms of online advertising. Defined as advertising that matches the form and function of the platform upon which it appears, native advertising is more closely integrated into the content of a web page (to the extent that it often serves as the primary content of a web page). Native advertising takes a number of forms including in-feed ads, search ads, recommendation widgets and promoted listings. Native advertising may be sourced directly from advertisers or obtained via number of native advertising companies. When using a third party to source native advertising it is important to review the content for quality and relevance.

Chapter 17

17. An Overview of BlockAdBlock, AdSorcery and AdBlock X

For web publishers looking for an alternative approach to the manual implementation of ad blocking detection and management, a number of ready to use services are available. Three such services are BlockAdBlock, AdSorcery and AdBlock X, an overview of each will be covered in this chapter.

17.1 BlockAdBlock

BlockAdBlock (http://www.blockadblock.com) is a free service that allows you to very quickly create custom ad blocker handling code which can then be embedded in your website. The default code provided by this website is designed to detect when an ad blocker is in use by a website visitor and repeatedly displays the dialog shown in Figure 17-1 until the ad blocker is disabled by the visitor:

Figure 17-1

If the default appearance and behavior of the detection script does not meet your requirements, the script can be customized as follows:

- **Block Mode** – Forces the visitor to disable ad blocking before access to the website is granted.
- **Nag Mode** – Makes only one request to the visitor to disable ad blocking before allowing unrestricted access.
- **Block Screen Delay** – The number of seconds after the visitor arrives on the web page before the block screen dialog is displayed.
- **Block Screen Text** – Allows the text of the block screen to be changed. A range of pre-configured text options are also available for selection.
- **Block Screen Display Options** – Allows the block screen color palette to be customized.
- **BlockAdBlock Branding** – By default the web page on which the block screen appears will also display the BlockAdBlock logo in the lower left hand corner of the page. This image can be replaced with a small text link indicating that you are using BlockAdBlock code.
- **Legal Text Options** – Optional legal text to be included within the ad detection code. This text does not appear within the block screen.
- **Analytics Integration** – Allows a Google Analytics event to be triggered each time the block screen is displayed to a site visitor.

Certainly, BlockAdBlock allows for the quick creation of ad block detection and ad blocker removal requests with an extensive range of options. If you need to quickly implement this type of behavior on your website this is a good approach. BlockAdBlock does, however, have some drawbacks in comparison to implementing your own code:

- The BlockAdBlock code is obfuscated which makes it impossible to make custom changes beyond those offered through the BlockAdBlock website.
- The code obfuscation makes it difficult to know exactly what the code is doing. Cautious web publishers may be reluctant to put code on a website without knowing what it is doing.
- A greater range of behavior options is available to you if you implement your own code (such as the ability to display the request dialog after a number of pages have been viewed or forcing the visitor to wait a specified period of time before the dialog can be dismissed).
- Analytics options are limited to counting how many times the block screen is displayed. No option is available to track how many visitors opted to disable ad blocking.
- It is not possible to entirely remove the BlockAdBlock branding from the blocking screen.

17.2 AdSorcery

AdSorcery (*http://www.adsorcery.com*) also provides a pre-built solution for handling ad blocking, though with a greater range of options than that offered by BlockAdBlock. Most significantly, AdSorcery provides the option to charge for access to the page and to run alternate ads. In order to use AdSorcery you will need to register to receive a login and password. Once registered, AdSorcery provides the following options:

- Request that site visitors turn off ad blocking.
- Deny website access to visitors until ad blocking is disabled.
- Require payment via credit card from customers using ad blocking in order to gain site access.
- Run alternate ads (either your own or those provided by AdSorcery) to visitors using ad blocking.

The AdSorcery dashboard provides a number of different ad blocking dialogs (an example of which is shown in Figure 17-2) from which to choose, all of which can be configured with your own wording, appearance effects (such as sliding and fading) and logo:

CompanyLogo

Please whitelist us on your ad blocker

We known ads suck. But this site is ad-supported & we need money to keep it running. We removed all the bad ads. Help us by whitelisting our site now.

No, I don't want to pay for this content

Figure 17-2

In addition to the appearance of the request dialog, the following additional configuration options are also available:

- Display request dialog only after a visitor has viewed a specified number of pages.
- Display request dialog only after a visitor has spent a specified number of seconds on the site.
- Specify the number of times the request is displayed per visitor.
- Restrict the number of times the dialog can be dismissed by a visitor.
- Require the visitor to wait a specified number of seconds before the dialog can be dismissed.

An Overview of BlockAdBlock, AdSorcery and AdBlock X

In terms of requiring payment from site visitors using ad blocking, AdSorcery presents an initial dialog which may be customized to request that the visitor either disable ad blocking or pay a specified amount for ad free access to the site. If the user chooses to pay for access, the dialog shown in Figure 17-3 will appear seeking credit card information:

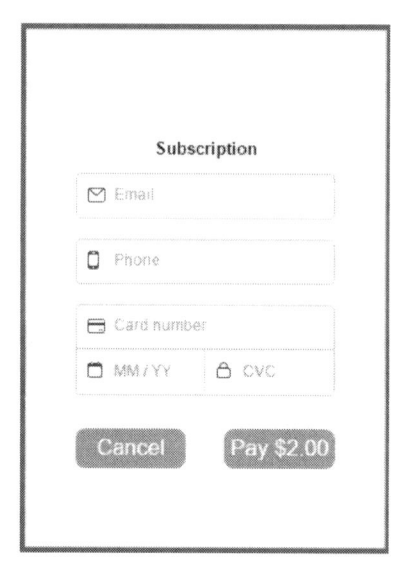

Figure 17-3

The current subscription options available with AdSorcery allow access for 1, 6 or 12 months. Existing subscribers will be able to bypass the blocking dialog on future visits to the site by entering the email address associated with their subscription.

17.3 **AdBlock X**

AdBlock X (*http://www.adblockx.com*) takes the form of a WordPress plugin or JavaScript code that works in conjunction with the AdBlock X portal (for which it is necessary to register in order to gain access).

Once AdBlock X has been implemented within a website, the AdBlock X portal (Figure 17-4) provides detailed statistics relating to visitor behavior:

An Overview of BlockAdBlock, AdSorcery and AdBlock X

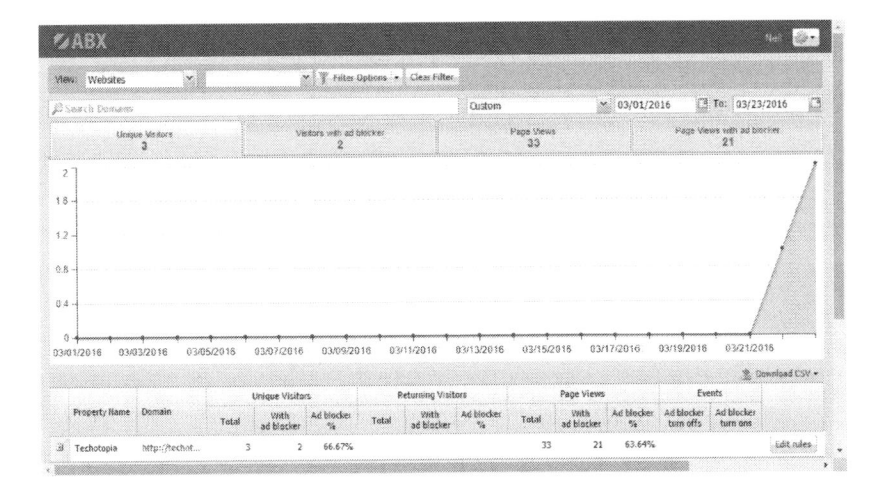

Figure 17-4

AdBlock X gathers data points such as the number of unique visitors, page views, ratio of visitors using ad blocking and whether visitors are using desktop or mobile devices. In fact, AdBlock X provides a range of filtering options allowing for detailed analysis of the data.

In addition to providing analytical data, AdBlock X also allows sets of rules to be implemented to control the way in which your website responds to ad blocking. Figure 17-5, for example, shows the AdBlock X rule editor configured to persistently request that ad blocking be turned off, with the request appearing every 3 page views and automatically closing after 10 seconds:

Figure 17-5

121

Multiple rules may be configured for a single domain, allowing the response to change based on criteria such as whether the visitor is using a mobile device while accessing the website.

The ad blocker responses available with AdBlock X allow for extensive configuration ranging from frequency of request to denying access to ad blocking visitors.

A particularly interesting option allows different content to be displayed within the web page depending on whether ad blocking is enabled. This involves the use of two different <div> tags. One is used as a wrapper around the content to be displayed to visitors using ad blocking and the other the regular content. The AdBlock X code will automatically toggle between the two content versions depending on whether an ad blocker is detected. AdBlock X refers to this as "content toggling" and suggests that it be used to show only the first part of the page content as a teaser to ad blocking visitors.

Once response filters have been implemented, statistics are also recorded for the number of visitors that turned off ad blocking.

AdBlock X is continuing to evolve and additional features may already have been implemented since this book was published.

17.4 Summary

While there is greater flexibility and control in implementing your own code and data gathering techniques for the management of ad blocking, a number of services have entered the market which will provide much of this functionality for you. Previous chapters have introduced the services offered by PageFair. In this chapter we have covered three other such services in the form of BlockAdBlock, AdSorcery and AdBlock X.

Chapter 18

18. Useful WordPress Plugins

In addition to the services outlined in the previous chapter, a number of useful plugins are available for managing ad blocking when using WordPress. Many of the plugins do little more than detect the presence of an ad blocker and respond by displaying a request that the blocker be disabled. Additionally, a number of ad blocking related plugins have been neglected by the original developer and are now rendered obsolete by changes in the ad blocking technology. There is even a plugin that, on detecting absence of an ad blocker, recommends to the visitor that one be installed (not a plugin we anticipate being popular with web publishers). With this caveat, this chapter will provide a summary of some of the plugins that were tested and known to work at the time of writing.

Other plugins can be found by searching the WordPress plugin catalog which may be accessed by opening the WordPress dashboard and selecting the *Plugins -> Add New* menu option.

18.1 Ad Blocking Detector

This plugin provides an easy way to implement ad reinsertion when running a WordPress based website. When added to a WordPress installation, this plugin detects the presence of an ad blocker and displays alternate content in place of the blocked ad. Unfortunately the popularity of this plugin has made it a target for the ad blocker community and what was once a simple installation now requires additional steps in order to make the plugin work. If you are willing to take these extra steps, however, then this is still a useful plugin.

18.2 Ad Blocking Advisor

The Ad Blocking Advisor plugin provides a quick way to detect the presence of an ad blocker and display a notification bar (Figure 18-1) requesting that the blocker be disabled.

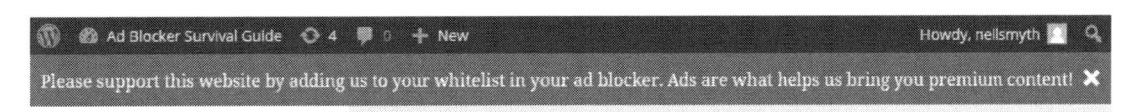

Figure 18-1

The Ad Blocker Advisor plugin includes a range of configuration options allowing for customization of the position, color and message. The plugin may also be configured to use a cookie to control the frequency (in days) within which a visitor sees the message.

18.3 AdBlock X

The WordPress plugin that accompanies the AdBlock X service as outlined in the chapter entitled *An Overview of BlockAdBlock, AdSorcery and AdBlock X*.

18.4 BlockAlyzer

The BlockAlyzer plugin is a quick and easy way to gather statistics on the number of visitors to your WordPress based website that are using an ad blocker. Once installed, BlockAlyzer adds an *adblock stats* menu to the WordPress dashboard Tools menu which, when selected, displays statistical information about page views, unique visitors and the percentage of ad blocker usage in each category as illustrated in Figure 18-2:

Figure 18-2

18.5 Summary

A number of WordPress plugins are available that provide and quick and easy way to take some basic first steps in dealing with ad blocking. A number of other plugins are available for use with WordPress, but were found to no longer work, or duplicated the functionality of those listed above.

19. Glossary

Acceptable Ads - A program initiated by Eyeo, the company behind AdBlock Plus which allows ads that meet certain criteria to be displayed even when AdBlock Plus is enabled.

Ad reinsertion – The process of replacing blocked ad space with alternate content, typically in the form of a house ad or an appeal to the visitor to turn off ad blocking.

Bait content – Content embedded within a web page and used by ad blocker detection code for the specific purpose of attracting attention of an ad blocker.

Blacklist – A list of web page element and ad server address filters used by ad blocking technology to identify the ad related content within a web page to block.

Cookie - Allows websites to store information on the computer of the visitor browsing your website.

DEAL – An acronym devised by the Interactive Advertising Bureau representing the recommended steps for dealing with ad blocking (detect ad blocking, explain the value exchange that advertising enables, ask for changed behavior and lift restrictions or limit access in response to consumer choice).

EasyList – The filter list used by AdBlock Plus and some other ad blocking solutions to identify ad elements in a web page and the addresses of known ad servers.

False positive – When ad blocker detection code falsely identifies the presence of an ad blocker when one is not actually in use.

Facebook Pixel – A fragment of code embedded into the pages of a web site which enables the site owner to target website visitors with Facebook advertisements.

House ads - Ads that a company displays on its own website, house ads are commonly used to promote products or services. House ads may also be used in conjunction with ad reinsertion.

Glossary

LEAN - An acronym devised by the Interactive Advertising Bureau representing the concept of making online adverts leaner, safer and less invasive (light, encrypted, ad choices support, non-invasive/non-disruptive).

Minified JavaScript – Also referred to as compression, this is the process of reducing the size of JavaScript code so that it downloads faster when a web page loads. Unlike obfuscation, compression does not typically obscure the intent and purpose of the code.

Obfuscation – Refers to a technique that is commonly used to obscure the operation and intent of code contained within a web page. JavaScript obfuscation can be used to hide the intent of ad blocker detection and response code.

Native advertising – Defined by Wikipedia as a type of advertising, usually online but feasibly elsewhere, that matches the form and function of the platform upon which it appears.

Whitelist – A list of exceptions to the blacklist. An ad blocker user can choose to add a website to their personal ad blocker whitelist so that ads are visible when visiting that site even when the blocker is enabled.

Index

A

Acceptable Ads · 99, 125
    approval process · 103
    content criteria · 102
    controversy · 100
    PageFair · 105
    placement criteria · 101
    pros and cons of · 101
    size criteria · 102
Access Denial · 81
    risks associated with · 82
Ad Blocker
    detection · 15
    detection code · 16
    types of · 9
Ad Blocker Lists · 12
Ad Blocker Removal
    controlling request frequency · 73
    requests · 59
Ad Blocking
    how it works · 9
    overview of · 9
Ad Blocking Advisor Plugin · 123
Ad Blocking Detector Plugin · 123
Ad reinsertion · 41, 125
    content recommendations · 45
    implementation · 42
    limitations of · 42
    overview · 41

Ad Servers
    blocking access to · 10
Adblock Warning Removal List · 60
AdBlock X · 120
AdBlock X Plugin · 124
AdSorcery · 118
Advertising Elements
    hiding of · 9

B

Bait content · 125
Bait Content · 15
Blacklist · 125
BlockAdBlock · 21, 117
blockAdBlock.check() function · 22
blockadblock.js file · 21
BlockAlyzer Plugin · 124
Bootstrap framework
    Modal dialog · 64
Bootstrap JavaScript framework · 61

C

CoinTent.com · 56
Cookie · 125
    domain setting · 75
    expiration · 75
    Name / Value pair · 75

Index

    path setting · 75
    structure of · 75
Cookies · 74

D

DEAL · 6, 125
Denying Access · 82
Dialog
    button clicks · 67
    timeout delay · 68
    tracking code · 68
Dialog Request
    displaying a · 64
Digital Goods
    selling · 51
Document Object Model · 9
DOM · 9
    programming interface · 10
Donation Requests · 53

E

EasyList · 12, 15, 45, 60, 61, 125
Errata · 2
Expiration-based Requests · 76
Eyeo GmbH · 99

F

Facebook
    Ad Manager · 54
    custom audience · 55
Facebook Advertising · 53
Facebook Pixel · 54, 125
Fading Effect · 95
False positive · 125

G

Google Analytics
    account creation · 29
    analyzing segment data · 37
    event triggering · 31
    Segments · 34
    tracking adblocker use · 28
    viewing events · 32

I

IAB · 6, 7, 81, 112
In-Ad · 115
In-Feed Ads · 112
Interactive Advertising Bureau · 6

J

JavaScript compression · 49
JavaScript console
    displaying · 11
JavaScript Cookie · 74
JavaScript Obfuscation · 47
    how it works · 48
JavaScript Obfuscator · 50
jQuery JavaScript library · 26

L

Leaky Paywall plugin · 56
LEAN · 7, 126
linear gradient · 96

M

Mailing List
    building · 53

Index

Minified JavaScript · 126
Minifying · 49
mobile apps · 57
Modal Plugin · 64

N

Native Ad Content
    types of · 112
Native advertising · 111, 126
    Implementing · 115
    In-Ad · 115
    In-Feed Ads · 112
    overview · 111
    promoted listings · 114
    recommendation widgets · 113
    Search Ads · 113
NavBar component · 61
navbar-fixed-bottom class · 63
navbar-fixed-top class · 63
Notification Bar
    displaying a · 61

O

Obfuscation · 47, 126
Outbrain · 116

P

Page Views
    removal request based on · 77
PageFair
    acceptable ads · 105
    network ads · 107
    pros and cons · 109
    tracking adblocking with · 25
PageFair Ads
    creating · 105

Paywall.com · 56
Physical Merchandise
    selling · 52
PigeonPaywall.com · 56
Premium Content · 56
Promoted Listings · 114

R

Recommendation Widgets · 113

S

Search Ads · 113
setTimeout() function · 17
ShareThrough · 116
Sponsorship · 56
SubscriptionGenuis.com · 56

T

Taboola · 116
Tracking Scripts
    blocking of · 39
Truncated Content · 91

V

Visitor Response Rate
    tracking · 85

W

Web Page Content
    truncation · 91
Whitelist · 94, 126
window.location.reload() function · 83
WordPress · 18, 20, 26, 28, 29, 120, 123, 124

Index

footer.php · 19
header.php · 26
Leaky Paywall plugin · 56

Plugins · 123
Templates · 26

Printed in Great Britain
by Amazon